Mentored by a Maverick
A Memoir of Rob Moore

Robert Stanley Moore and Robin K. Moore

ROB and ROBIN MOORE

Praise for Rob Moore, His Life and His Mentorship

Rob was a great mighty man. If he could speak to us right now, he would say, "Thank you for the time we had together. Don't take a single day for granted. Be a God-first, kingdom-focused man. Love your wife. Lead your family. Live to give and advance God's kingdom in the earth. Fight the good fight. Prove yourself." I loved this man.

Keith Craft
Lead Pastor, Elevate Life Church, Frisco, Texas

As a young man, I realized Rob just had so much trust for young people. He trusted me to lead his kids, he trusted me to have something to say to them and even in my youth he trusted that God would use me to do something great. He would often ask me to lay hands on him and pray for him. It was his obstinate belief that made me more of a believer myself in what God could do through me. In the face of any obstacle he believed that God was going to be God, that God was going to do what he said he was going to do and that was pivotal in my faith.

Josh Craft
Pastor, Elevate Life Church, Frisco, Texas

A MUST read book - Rob was the true definition of a Maverick! Bold, independent thinking, a real man's man, and a Warrior for God. He taught us all 'How to leave a legacy.' He cared about everyone. He was my friend, and my brother, and his legacy will live on forever!

Mark Blum
Evangelism Pastor, Elevate Life Church, Frisco, Texas

I got to spend some significant time with Rob and hear some pretty incredible stories about his life. This is what you hold in your hands right now. I also got enough time to discover what an incredible man he was. What I know is that Rob Moore LIVED! The word of God says that Jesus came that we might have abundant life and this man lived more life confined in a chair than most men will live in perfectly good health. Rob is an inspiration to us all. He didn't allow his disability to define him. He really did life to the fullest. He never allowed the opinion of others to dictate what he was going to do before his God. You can tell a lot about a person from the fruit he leaves behind. His legacy is enormous.

Clay Jones
Pastor, Elevate Life Church, Frisco, Texas

As Rob Moore's first-born son, I was his favorite test case and field study for all his consulting matters. I consider myself a far better man for abiding by his words - and to this day I still seek his wisdom daily.

Jordan Dallas Moore
Rob and Robin's Son

I want to thank and honor my dad for being my best friend, my leader, my protector, my teacher and my example. He was known for not only being very wise but also being very young at heart and full of fun. I feel he has put that same spirit over my life. It is the greatest compliment in the world for me to hear someone say that I remind them of my father.

Jeremiah Moore
Rob and Robin's Son

Rob always seemed to look for and find the best in all situations, even when the worst was displayed. He had an unshakeable, unstoppable God-fidence. He was strong and faithful and fought the good fight of faith. He was truly a mighty man of the highest order and one of my heroes.

Chuck Phelps

Brace yourself! Your life is about to be eternally impacted by true stories of Holy Spirit encounters with Rob Moore. Through this man, I was challenged, taught, and inspired to know the Lord more deeply. His intimate fellowship and walk with Christ inspired me to live out my faith in the same manner.

Raymond Najera
Men's Group Leader

Rob could make you feel like a slacker. He could! He didn't have to say anything. He would just show up. To everything. On time. Seriously. You have no idea what the struggle was on a daily basis for him just to show up, but his presence pushed us to be better men. I never, not once, in all the years that I knew him, heard an excuse from Rob. Not one time. He just was faithful. Faithful with his money, faithful with his time. Faithful with his family. You never knew him as less, always MOORE. What a great example to follow.

Scott Unclebach

Rob Moore, I salute you for a race well run! If following Jesus was a crime, there was plenty of evidence to convict you. You left a true legacy in your family to elevate them to allow them to exceed you. Well done, good and faithful servant.

Mitch Edland

To me, Rob Moore was the incarnate Apostle Paul, spreading the Word of God and love to everyone he met.
Serge Sokol

I've been a friend of Rob's for years and I can tell you that he's one of the most godly and wise men that I've ever met. His counsel has always been highly regarded and widely sought out. Therefore, I'd highly recommend this book to everyone.
Sean Hyman
Financial Author, Speaker and Pastor

Rob was always a Winner! I couldn't have wished for a better son-in-law. He made my daughter Robin happy for more than 30 years. They gave us four amazingly awesome, intelligent grandchildren and raised them to be faithful, honest, respectful, well mannered, educated and self-sufficient. This was accomplished not just through teaching, but also by living the example. As the saying goes, Rob not only talked the talk, he walked the walk. I am proud that he was a part of our family and left these words for us.
Steven W. Neighbors
Robin's Dad

Meeting Rob for the first time I knew that I had just met a modern day apostle. Then after traveling with him across the country I would see that same reception from everyone he encountered. Rob saw his disability as an ability to let the Lord shine through him!
Chris Shaffer

Rob spent hours talking to me about life. He taught me to be a man after God's own heart. He was a living example of a spiritual being having a human experience. He led me to being transformed into a better man.
Shawn Nelson

I celebrate Rob and his kingdom perspective.
Brian Baker

Maverick is saying it mildly! In our conversations together, Rob Moore's calm demeanor with a confident peace spoke volumes. You could see his fire, love and obedience he had with Jesus. He was a loving warrior with a passion to change the lives of others by his obedience in his own life. It was awe-inspiring. As you hear him speak of how the Holy Spirit moved in and through his life, especially when it wasn't easy, you will be inspired also to press in further to all that God has for you.
John Lancaster

Ironically, the substance of my relationship with Rob Moore began and ended with a kiss on his forehead in a hospital emergency room. In the six years in between, I learned more from Rob about what it meant to truly be a disciple of Jesus Christ than any time before or after. Rob was my best friend. I learned how to be a best friend from Rob as he constantly sought to be his BEST so that he would bring out the BEST in me.
Pat Feyen

Rob Moore was a man of great faith, strength and vision. He truly had a servant's heart and was an inspiration to all he met. It was an honor to know and learn from him. This book will allow you to do the same.
Keth Edmonson

Rob was unshakeable, had a great sense of humor and was a get'r done kind of guy.
Mark Berndt

Being new in my walk with God, Rob was the finest real live person I have met that opened my eyes and mind through hearing his experiences with the power of the Holy Spirit working through a human being. Just listening to him as he shared the numerous occasions he would witness, play the part or just be the miracle was amazing. It was all due to this faithful servant leading in a walk with our Lord and Savior.
Ricardo Henry

Rob was in this world, but his spirit was not from this world. I sensed a disciple's presence though his parable-like teachings will continue to be an inspiration to spread God's Holy Word. The broad smile from this wheelchair-bound warrior at 6:30am made it all worth the effort. Rob - a modern day Paul who taught incessantly.
Dwayne Brinkley

I have had three mentors in my 60+ years. One taught me how to run a successful business. One helped me find the true meaning of God. Rob showed me how to love life.
Mark Zidell

Rob Moore meant the world to me and many other men. He was my Paul, a true spiritual father. He poured into me several times, keeping me from making serious mistakes in my marriage. He will always be remembered and revered.
Neal Stokey

Since hearing of Rob's passage from this earth, I have been celebrating in my heart, the life he had on this earth. He was a true friend to me and many others. HIs courageous heart will live on through those he loved and touched. Looking forward to seeing him again in his new home!
Mark Hsi
Pastor

I will always remember Rob's positive attitude in the midst of adversity. He was an inspiration to me.
Jack Nordgren
Pastor, Hope Chapel South Shore

Rob and I had a love/hate relationship. He loved me with gentle kindness by nailing me between the eyes with truth. I hated that he was always right when he challenged me. It truly made me a better man and I will always love him for that.
Don Dryden

Wow. Rob was (and still is in heaven) an amazing mighty man whose obedience enabled him to be blessed to be a blessing to others. He poured into me and let the Holy Spirit flow through him in a way that is very hard to find. He taught me a lot in the time I knew him and had great miracle moments in my life that directly related to him. God used him to build my faith and the fruit of his family and legacy pushes me to live stronger for God. I will always love and miss him. But, I will see him again!
Steve Cortes

I am proud to have been a friend of Rob's. If not for knowing both of you I would have never met the love of my life over 30 years ago!
Dave Dirren
Formerly of R & D Construction

Although someone else introduced me to Christ, it was Rob that led me to believe it was true. It was Rob, after all, who baptized me. I will always remember our brief, but convincing conversation that left no doubt that I needed to be baptized. That was Rob. When he spoke, it often had deep meaning and a profound way of convincing you that what he was saying was true and often urgent. At least for the Kingdom of God.
Mike Petrovich

I really am glad to have known Rob Moore. Great encourager and lover of God and the people around him. Thank you Lord for using Rob in the lives of so many people including me.
Wendell Elento

Rob is a consummate storyteller whose life epitomizes the love of Jesus Christ. From the moment I met Rob we bonded as brothers and had the privilege of sharing in the unveiling of each other's life stories. Always with a sense of humor, he delivers His Story in an engaging way.
Michael A. Valentino

I hope and pray that I can take everything Rob taught me and showed me into my life. And bring that into my new marriage. I strive to be half the man that Rob was so I can be a good servant to The Lord and leader to my family.
Kapono Ho'opii

A man's man that truly put kingdom first and his family's needs above his own. Rob was a man that was an example to others of what a "man after God's own heart" looked like. This book will show you the man that is Rob Moore.
Thomas O'Dell

He was a close brother to me and he made me realize that every day was a God made day and shared so many of his past experiences and he made me become a better Warrior!
Jonathan Best

Rob is the truest example of a man of God that I have personally known. He was wise, humble, honoring and bold. Father to the fatherless, he was true to the Word and had a sense of humor that could only come from God. You will enjoy this book.
Austin O'Dell

As a very wise, very amazing friend of mine Rob Moore used to say, "I don't belong here, I am only on this earth for just a sliver of time, just passing by." Although he lived for such an awesome purpose, he was always "just passing by."
Michael Angel Ramirez

Rob Moore is an amazing man who preached into my life through our Thursday night men's group. He always had a way of looking at things that made you open your mind, and I loved the time I got to spend getting to know him. Can't wait to see him again one day, He will always have a place in my heart!
Ryan Fitzpatrick

"I'm not afraid to fail. I know that if I fail, I fall in the palm of God and therefore it is never fatal" – Rob Moore. Through the wisdom and life lessons that Rob shared with me, I had the courage to quit my full-time job and pursue my dreams of starting a special needs business. Today, my income is higher than it's ever been in my life and my wife no longer has to work. Rob Moore (who gave me the vision for my ministry, Special Strong) always told me, "Slowing down is sometimes the best way to speed things up." To be honest, I never really believed it. In this new season of my life, I am starting to see the truth behind this wisdom.
Daniel Stein

Rob! I honor you today to celebrate your life by striving to be a better man. Your WARRIOR legacy lives on through your family and the Mighty Men of ELC.
John Vakidis

Rob Moore, a " maverick cowboy" rode into my life in 2005 with guns a'blazing, full of truth and grace as a reflection of the Lord. He set up camp, rode the trails of life with me, walked the walk, then rode into the sunset to his heavenly Dad. He might be gone but through this book, he's riding on.

J.D. Smith
Pastor, CitiImpact Ministries and Disaster Relief

Rob I will never forget our discussions at the coffee shop talking about how we can do a better job about sharing Jesus with others. Thank you for your wisdom and making me better! I HONOR YOU!!! See you in Heaven my friend. Much LOVE!!!!

Blake Porter

My Captain My Captain, the light shines so bright in you. I wasn't blinded but drawn to it. You humbled me and challenged me weekly. I love you for that. Not many men I would let mentor me but I was so drawn to you because the spirit was in you greatly. Thank you my mentor, my brother, my warrior and truly my friend.

Jason Poncio

Rob Moore reminds us to trust in the powerful truth that with God we don't have to let our thinking be limited. By obeying Him, and living beyond the boundaries we set in our own mind with passion, God can do exceedingly, abundantly more then we can ask, think or imagine! Thank you for the Honor and reminding me what a gift he was in my life!

Kenny Gammons

Rob spoke of things he had in his life that he wanted in mine. Rob did these things well: A Brother, Friend, Teacher, Son, Husband, Father, Mentor, Messenger, Equipper, Leader, Entrepreneur, Motivator, Maverick. Rob was: Disciplined, Loving, Grace filled, Accountable, Dependable, Joyful, Content. Let Rob speak to you.
Wayne Katayama

I can't say enough about what a great witness Rob Moore was by the way he lived his life. If you ever looked Rob in the eye, you know that he was filled with the Holy Spirit and overflowing with love. His pain and suffering was never known by others as he was sowing into them. He has left a true legacy with his family as they have the same characteristics he had. His last words to me were, "I love you, man."
Darrell McCauley

Rob was a unique man in that his focus seemed to be about bringing the best out of the loved ones around him. I remember a few times when he challenged me personally to get serious about my passion. My passion is art and some of my best works came right after his discussions with me. I was able to share with him some of those works so he could tangibly see the difference he had made in my life. After his passing, I had the honor of creating his image on canvas for his family. Thank you, Rob, for the motivation and the memories.
Corbin Runnels

Rob's relationship with my father is what I remember the most. Once Rob and my dad grew close with each other, my whole family dynamic changed. He was able to love my mother and I like never before because of the amazing example Rob led as a father and husband.

Darian Runnels

ROB and ROBIN MOORE

Mentored by a Maverick
A Memoir of Rob Moore

Robert Stanley Moore and Robin K. Moore

ROB and ROBIN MOORE

Copyright

DEDICATION

To Rob Moore:
You were my "E" ticket ride.
Love, Robin.

To the Family and Friends of Rob Moore:
He fought the good fight for your benefit.

And a special "Thank You" to the Mighty Men of Elevate Life Church
in Frisco, TX who listened and loved Rob, and who continue the legacy
of being Mentored by a Maverick.

Table of Contents

ROB and ROBIN MOORE

INTRODUCTION

"Something's burning!"

As a boy, I felt "the maverick" running wild in my veins. My heroes were the gunfighters of the 1960's spaghetti westerns and I reveled in their daredevil manhood. Like them, no one could tell me what to do and I pushed the envelope in every way. As I grew into a man I always felt like a leader, but didn't necessarily see anyone I thought was worth following. I needed someone to follow that encouraged my willingness to be marked as different and set apart from the crowd. To really man up, I needed to be led where was I weakest. In righteousness, truthfulness, boldness, faithfulness, loyalty and authenticity. I needed someone to lead me that would "tell me like it was" and speak to me in a language I could understand. Not to tame me, but to bring the best out of me. Truly, I needed another maverick to lead me away from destruction and into life.

Maybe you feel 'the maverick' running in your veins, too. Whether life is currently good, bad or ugly (or if any of this rings true), I want to invite you to experience my journey of aligning with the ultimate mentor for ALL mavericks. In these pages you will meet a Mentor who able to inspire the wildest of us.

Robert S. Moore

"After a season of writing children's books, Rob asked me to do some writing with him. Partnering with my husband's superb storytelling, we began to chronicle his amazing journey of an impossible life. Story after story of the miraculous hand of

God in our life evolved into our joint work, **Mentored By A Maverick.** It is a privilege to share his legacy with the world.

His love for 1960's spaghetti westerns, the maverick gunslinger cowboy and all things virile and manly are the backbone to his story. Mostly he would want this written to prove to people that a man can love the Lord and not be a sissy...

In capturing Rob's voice, I hope you hear an even clearer voice ringing in your ears as you read---the voice of the Maverick Mentor calling out to you.

Robin K. Moore

CHAPTER 1

The Maverick Mentor

Like every other boy who grew up in the 1960's, I loved watching westerns. Some kids wanted to be pitchers or pilots. Some wanted to be firemen or freedom fighters. Not me. Whether it be Gunsmoke or Bonanza, The Rifleman, Maverick or Rawhide, my heroes wore cowboy hats, cowboy boots, and cowhide jackets, carried six shooters on their gun belts and had an intimidating scowl. My heroes were larger than life and completely in control. Although the shootouts between the good guys and the bad guys were pretty exciting, there was always one guy in a western that really intrigued me: The Maverick. Mysterious and all-knowing, it was the unbranded maverick who I identified with and who represented the best of manhood to me.

The word "maverick" comes from an old Texas cattle baron. In the 1800's, Samuel A. Maverick owned a lot of cattle and he let them roam around Texas without a brand seared into their skins. On the range, you usually found cattle already branded or it was probably a "maverick" and belonged to Sam.

To me, a maverick is an original rebel who doesn't do what is expected. He is the guy that isn't scared to cross the line of conformity. Although it originally referred to unbranded cattle that strayed from the herd, it also began to apply to a person who did not follow the thinking of an established group, who rebelled against the herd mentality. Because he made an independent stand from his associates, a maverick made everyone stop and think differently.

Since the time of my boyhood, mavericks had made their mark on me. I loved the old "Maverick" television series and the 1990 movies with the same name starring James Garner. Fender Instruments built a Maverick guitar which I coveted as a teenager. George Thorogood and the Destroyers put out an album in 1985 called "Maverick" which played on my cassette deck for hours. In my lifetime I also enjoyed a great surf spot called "Mavericks."

Currently I follow the Dallas Mavericks, an NBA basketball team from Dallas, Texas. Interestingly, there is also a Maverick County in South Texas near the Mexico border. Heck! Even my Apple OS X named their computer operating system "Mavericks."

I have to admit, not all mavericks have left a positive connotation in my memory, though. For example, there is an electro-optically guided air-to-ground tactical missile called a Maverick. When I met my wife in 1982, she drove an ugly little lime green Ford Maverick with olive green interior. I nicknamed it the Ford "mad wreck." But overall, the idea of a maverick always made a positive mark in my life and stirred my soul, leaving me wanting more.

During the era of the spaghetti westerns on the silver screen in the 1960's, the maverick became even more legendary in my young mind. All my neighborhood friends knew "A Fistful of Dollars" starred the mysterious "Man With No Name." The distinct trilling whistle from the musical score by Ennio Morricone still jars me down memory lane as I think back to when I saw the other two movies of the trilogy "For a Few Dollars More" and "The Good, the Bad, and the Ugly." The boy in me could not get enough of this maverick cowboy.

I can still remember the moment when the nameless cowboy, played by Clint Eastwood, first filled the screen. As actor Jim Carrey once said, "I think the reason he had no name is so that we can all insert our own." From the moment he entered the frame, I was mesmerized by this commanding figure.

His low-slung gun belt and that fringed poncho jacket looked so incredibly unique and yet intimidating. From the metallic jangle of spurs on those well worn boots to that iconic weather-beaten hat tilted at an angle, I was drawn into his steely-eyed gaze. He was all the man I dreamed to be.

My neighborhood posse ran around all summer pulling our six shooters from our hips and looking for bad guys while imitating that trebling whistle. We all played "wild, wild west" for hours on end with those cowboy influences as our heroes. The 'Maverick Cowboys' had my attention.

As I look back and ponder...why cowboys? Today, I think they represented manhood to me. Even though the world has changed a lot in the last quarter century, I have found the values of the cowboy has stayed consistent over the years. Things like:

- ✓ Be faithful.
- ✓ Don't inquire into a person's past. Take the measure of a man for what he is today.
- ✓ Defend yourself when necessary.

- ✓ Don't talk much. Save your breath for breathing or speaking truth.
- ✓ Be loyal to the brand, your friends and those you ride with.
- ✓ Complaining is what whiners do.
- ✓ Always help somebody in need, even an enemy.
- ✓ Give people something to respect.
- ✓ Above all, be honorable.

Screenwriter John Fusco, author of the cowboy epic *Hidalgo*, wrote, "Times change, but the cowboy doesn't: While our culture might sell out; the cowboy stays true to his values (and his horse)." Fusco wrote. "Rock stars, rap stars, and movie stars come and go - loudly. The cowboy remains - quietly. There's a little bit of him in every American. That's why we need him."

Cowboys and all they stood for became my measure of a man. Although the cowboy mentored me as a boy, I quickly grew from a boy into a young man that was wise in my own eyes. I felt the maverick running wild in my veins and I reveled in my manhood. No one could tell me what to do and I pushed the envelope every way that I could.

It was going to take more than a mere cowboy to mentor my arrogant self. It was going to take a force to be reckoned with. It was going to take another maverick to tame me and make me want to earn his respect.

As a grown man, I always felt like a leader but didn't necessarily see anyone I thought was worth following. I needed a mentor that solved the problem, won the fight, and lived by a code of ethics. I needed to learn some mighty life lessons from a larger than life maverick who would mentor me with simple truths. I needed someone to lead me that would tell me like it was and speak to me in a language I could understand.

One night at my dining room table, a pastor invited me and my wife to pray to invite Jesus Christ to be our Lord and Savior. Wanting a successful mentor in this new walk of life, I began to assess the men around me in the church. I saw what I thought looked like a lot of sheep following a shepherd. However, sheep that liked being branded and stayed in the pen were not the type of men I wanted to mentor me. Was I wrong to want to remain a maverick? I craved for someone bold to follow. Someone who didn't necessarily play by the rules or follow the crowd of the establishment. I needed someone who wasn't afraid to shake people up and make them think. I didn't see many men like that in the church. I reached out to my pastor and he encouraged me to read the Scriptures.

When I began to read the Word of God, I found someone who really intrigued me. He was unbranded. This is what I loved about this man called 'Jesus' I had met in the Scriptures.

✓ He refused to answer to the established Pharisees (rulers) of the day, calling them vipers because of their snake-like duplicity. (Matthew 23).
✓ He was no stranger to crossing the line of conformity by healing people on a Sabbath day.
✓ He defied cultural taboos like talking to a Samaritan woman at a well.
✓ He took an independent stand by failing to fulfill the wishes of the townspeople to stone an adulterous woman.
✓ He didn't always do what people expected by telling a rich young man to give up everything.
✓ He went against the grain of common sense, inviting fisherman to come fish for men instead of the catch of the day.
✓ He made people think, asking them, "Who do YOU say I

am?"
- ✓ He did unpopular things by eating with sinners.
- ✓ He acted in an unorthodox way like sleeping in a boat that was being tossed in a storm.
- ✓ He even did the miraculous by walking on water and changing water to wine.

There was also a time when his own family went to take charge of him because they thought he was out of his mind. (Mark 3:21 NIV)

The more I read, the more I was really beginning to like this guy! I finally found my Maverick Mentor! His name was Jesus Christ. Seeing the maverick in Jesus made a connection to my soul and the maverick in me. Aha! That is who I wanted to be like. This maverick, Jesus. Finally, someone who understood my wildness, my edgy, rebellious bent. I finally humbled myself and asked this maverick Jesus to mentor me. He took the challenge seriously (a maverick always does) and I went for the ride of my life.

What he very clearly demonstrated to me was:

#1. He knows "Who" He rides for.

#2. He is always loyal to the brand.

Even in his maverick personality, Jesus always honored God the Father and kept his focus on His purpose. He showed me there is a difference between being a rebellious rebel and being a maverick with a purpose.

Over the years, Jesus has used the iconic spaghetti western cowboy to teach me more about Himself. My example of Clint Eastwood, James Garner, and the others prepared me to understand the lessons that Jesus Christ, my Lord, wanted to instill in me. He took my picture of the maverick to the next level.

Today, I have seasoned and matured. Like my mentor, I know who I ride for (God Almighty) and I am intensely loyal to my brand (Christianity). My mentor has taught me to clothe myself in the wardrobe of a maverick cowboy, complete with a:

- ✓ fringed leather jacket of righteousness,
- ✓ a gun belt of truthfulness,
- ✓ some bold boots of the gospel,
- ✓ a squint of faith,
- ✓ a cowboy hat (Stetson) of salvation and
- ✓ a six-shooter of the Spirit.

Some days I feel like I am walking around with a squint looking for an imaginary duel at high noon. "Do you feel lucky, punk? Go ahead, make my day."

Maybe you find yourself "on the outside looking in" at traditional church goers or yearning for a mentor who challenges and inspires you every day. Maybe you are looking for someone who understands the risk-taking, slightly rebellious, edgy side of you.

Maybe you feel 'the maverick' running in your veins, too. If any of those ring true, I want to invite you into these pages to experience my journey of trail riding with Jesus.

As I share my journey from 1960's boyhood to the best of manhood with you, my fellow maverick, I pray you are mentored too.

Round Up Questions:

1.) Who has been a hero to you? What qualities attracted you to them?

2.) What is your idea of a maverick? Can you describe a maverick that you have met?

3.) What values have you aimed to live by?

4.) Have you ever invited someone to mentor you? What was the experience like?

5.) Have you ever been a mentor for someone? How was the experience?

CHAPTER 2

"The Dog You Feed the Most"

The Mavericks

Bret and Bart Maverick were like my older brothers. I looked up to them, wanted to be like them, and hung out with them on a regular basis. Actually, they were actors in a television show I watched religiously. The Maverick Brothers were poker players from Texas who traveled all over the Old West and on the Mississippi riverboats, constantly getting into and out of life-threatening trouble of one sort or another, usually involving money, women, or both. They would typically find themselves weighing a financial gain against a moral dilemma. More often than not, their consciences trumped their wallets since both Mavericks were extremely ethical.

Bret and Bart's "Pappy", Beau Maverick, tried his best to mentor his boys. He was full of advice. One of the sons would frequently announce, "As my Pappy used to say..." followed by one of these witty comments:

- "Never cry over spilled milk, it could've been whiskey."
- "A coward dies a thousand deaths, a hero dies but one. I'd say a thousand to one is pretty good odds."
- And my favorite (because it reminds me of what my own pappy would say): "If you're ever served a rare steak that is intended for someone else, don't bother with ethical details - eat as much as you can before the mistake is discovered."

Pappy Beau was a wealth of witty comments or "Pappyisms."

Egged on by Bret and Bart, the natural maverick in me was racing in my veins at a young age, but I needed to be trained in how NOT to be wise in my own eyes. To become the man God intended for me to be it was going to take more than a few 'pappyisms'... a more mature spiritual maverick needed to be awakened.

Let's go back to the beginning...

It was an understatement to say I was wise in my own eyes as I came of age. Like many kids in the 1960's during the summer time, I was required to be out of the house all day and back home when the street lights came on. I took to the road each morning on my bike and I never looked back. I answered to no one and did as I pleased. Wise in my own eyes.

Every time I got in trouble in the neighborhood (usually for jumping my bike over Mrs. Cranston's garbage cans) my parents would take me to task to correct me. I would respond, "I know. I know." My dad would regularly say to me, "Son, you *think* you know; but you don't. I know."

After being corrected for my smart mouth, I would quip, "Dad, you taught me everything I know!" Then, I would get his other favorite line, "Boy, I did teach you everything you know. But, I didn't teach you everything that *I* know." Wise in my own eyes.

Most of my life I've looked and acted older than I was and this typically worked to my advantage. Unlike a lot of boys today, I was eager to drive and had my license and first car by my sixteenth birthday. I was unstoppable ...until the times I got in trouble as a teenager and had to answer to my dad. As I sat fumbling with my lame words in his presence, trying to justify my foolish actions, I would hear him say, "Son, you can't con a con man." Nope, he didn't buy my stories. He always could see right through my bravado. It was a picture of my future conversations with my Heavenly Father as well. I could never pull over anything on either one of them.

As a healthy adult male, I had been encouraged by my father to be my own man. I bought my first house at age 18 and moved out. I graduated college at 20 and was a project manager for a successful construction company. I bought my second house with my bride and didn't look to anyone for anything. I didn't like being told what to do, how to act, or what I should or should not say. I prided myself on my inability to be shepherded into the sheep pen. (Key word: pride) Even after I accepted Christ into my life, I did not see a single man in the Christian realm that I could identify with. Until I met this Maverick Jesus, in the Word of God.

Here on the pages of this ancient text, I saw a maverick in action. He pissed off the Pharisees so much they wanted to kill him. He confused the crowds (isn't that the carpenter's son?). He talked to his own friends in parables that he had to explain to them. Actually, the good Lord, was quite baffling, even to his own family. His cousin, John the Baptist, was not sure what to make of him asking, "Are you the one who is to come?" His own disciples were confused by his request to wash their feet. But he never acted without authority from God or to just promote himself. This was my new hero, my mentor, the man I chose to follow.

While my mentor had a knack for doing the unexpected, I began to see this as one of his trademarks. Things that made me go, "HMMM?" or made me marvel were more than mere coincidences. They were his hallmark - a sign that He was near and on the move. (I think the word HMMM stands for: "HallMark of Maverick Mentor".)

There were more than a few times that I looked at my life and sat shaking my head saying, "Hmmm." As a young buck, I had quite a few brushes with my own mortality. You think a near death experience or two would get my attention, but for my hard head - it took far more than one.

Close Calls

How many times have I had close calls with death? There have been several. Maybe that is why I have always felt the enemy's target on my back. I was marked. The enemy's tactics began early to take me out of the trail ride of life.

When I was sixteen years old, I was in a horrific head-on car crash that threw me through the windshield, knocked out my teeth, scarred my face, and broke my back. Doctors told me I should not have survived it. Miraculously, I lived. Hmmm.

While scuba diving in Hawaii, I was caught in a wicked current that runs off the coast of Oahu called the "Molokai Express." God sent a boat where there shouldn't ever be one to save me. Why didn't I go then? Hmmm.

Incredibly, I have also had a car transmission drop on

my head (that explains a lot), had a screwdriver narrowly miss my eye socket and impale my skull (I'm not scowling, that divot between my eyebrows is the scar), gotten broadsided in a Ford F150 extra cab (totaled it), landed a five car pile-up in a huge Chevy Suburban going 70 miles per hour on the Dallas Tollway (airbags saved my face that time), and slipped and fell on the floor a number of times (cracked some ceramic tiles with my skull). Hmmm.

I haven't even mentioned that my parents were told not to expect me to live through my preemie birth as they wheeled my mother into a Cesarean section in the early 1960's. Nor the two times while in elementary school I was hit by a car, or the innumerable bone breaks and fractures to my body during my boyhood.

Why, even Major League Baseball great, Jim Palmer, broke my eyeball socket bones when he beaned me in a game of catch with one of his fastballs.

You've heard the old adage: "If it weren't for bad luck, I'd have no luck at all." That is the perspective for a lot of people. Funny? Maybe. True? A lot of the time for some, but not for me.

If I thought like a victim I might wonder, "Lord, why did all those attempts on my life happen to me?"

Instead, the victor in me asks, "What kept me alive and well in spite of those close calls?" Hmmm.

The Word of God reminded me that we must "...be strong in the Lord and in His mighty power, putting on the full armor of God so that you can take your stand against the devil's schemes."

I believed the enemy of my soul was trying to take me out because I had something to bring. I figured, "God's not done with me, yet." To me, those close calls revealed that God had a purpose for my life as He kept me here for over fifty years. "For our struggle is not against flesh and blood, but against the rulers, against the authorities, against the powers of this dark world and against the spiritual forces of evil in the heavenly realms." (Ephesians 6:10-12)

I've learned that the closer your calls with death, the more you squeeze out of life. Not only have I had close calls with physical death, but even closer calls with the death of my fleshly self. As I died to myself and my agendas and my ways of doing things, the bolder I got and the harder I pressed for Jesus Christ.

Thoughts of my brushes with death were jumbling through my mind as I sat one morning in my church's espresso café. Fresh from the Sunday service, my spirit was soaring. I approached the counter and saw the coffee carafes lined up all neatly-labeled for my selection. That morning, my choices were LIGHT, MEDIUM or BOLD.

Hmmm. Any other day those would be coffee choices, but that morning I saw a natural/supernatural correlation from Jesus. In my life, I had already made my choice. I had gone from a "wise in my own eyes" punk to a wise old cowboy who boldly chose to be marked by his mentor. I didn't see myself as light or medium anymore. I was certainly bold.

Later that night, at 2:15 a.m., I woke up alert and ready. You might have thought my bold coffee affected my sleep, but I have learned through the years that it's the Lord's way of saying He wants to talk to me. In the still of the night, it is time for me to listen. While the house was quiet and my family slept, I found myself wheeling to my study. As I sat in the dark, my mentor began speaking things to my heart to put down in the light. From this quiet place, He called me to tell some tales of my struggles in learning to take the trademark, to write about the hallmarks, learning my lessons, and living my victories. He nudged me to write what lessons He, my Pappy, had taught me during my bold life. He wanted me to share how I went from "wise in my own eyes to the wise old man." By the light of my iPad, this old maverick cowboy began to type out his lessons learned...

Whose Team Are You On

I was newly saved – about forty days into my walk with God. Here's a glimpse of what my life was like at that time. My young wife and I were living in Arizona. I owned my own company and set my own hours and was my own man, so full of myself. As one of the youngest men ever to pass the exam for a General Contractor's license, I was making money hand over fist and we were living high on the hog. We were young, healthy, happy and lavishly indulging in the flesh. We had the grandest house in the neighborhood because we had upgraded everything possible and we drove expensive flashy sports cars. You've heard the phrase "keeping up with the Joneses"? – Well, we WERE the Joneses!

There was never a conflict in my soul until a decision to invite Christ into my heart woke up the spirit dog inside me. Those two dogs, the flesh dog (who had ruled for years) began to go to war with the newly awakened spirit. Trying to feed the spirit dog more, I intentionally set aside time to be with God to read his Word and to pray. For the first time, I was yielding myself, denying myself, restraining myself. I made a quiet place where I could go everyday to pray, read, and do my Christian thing – this place happened to be in the tropical paradise that was my backyard creation.

One afternoon I was in my quiet place (the hammock). I thought, "I have a pretty awesome thing going. Adding God to my picture is only going to make my life soar to another level." So I closed my eyes and I told God, "God, if you are who the Bible says you are, I want you on MY team." Happily, I laid back with a smile on my face like a guy who had just maneuvered an amazing deal.

In the peace and quiet of my backyard, God spoke audibly to my ears as if He was standing right in front of me. I clearly heard him say, "Son, I'm not on your team." What? God didn't want to be on my team? That rocked my world. I went from being Mr. Jones, the guy that was "all that and a bag of chips" to not even being the worthy of holding the bag. Twenty seconds of silence passed while I tried to encompass and encapsulate what had just happened. "I'm. Not. On. Your. Team." Those words pierced my heart! I was devastated and I felt abandoned.

Before I could blink, I heard Him audibly again. He said, "You are on MY team." I fell to the ground humbly on my knees. In an instant I understood. How prideful my viewpoint had been. The God of the universe had the ultimate team. My team? My team was laughable. My eyes were opened in one second. I had nothing to offer Him but myself. Earnestly, I pledged to Him, "Whatever You do, I'll do. And whatever You say, I'll say." I asked Jesus to be more than my Lord, I wanted Him to mentor me into being the kind of disciple that would bring Him glory. It was the decision that broke the enemy's hold over my life and put me under the protection of the Lord God Almighty. I learned I needed to remember who I rode for and to be loyal to the brand, not the other way around. Like old Samuel Maverick, my mentor did not brand me with a physical mark but

I was all His nonetheless.

That moment is what started me on this journey. It was that moment; when my soul was awakened and the tide turned from being under control of the flesh man to yielding to the spirit man. It's from that spiritual awakening that all of these stories come. That was the beginning, the root of discerning God's voice and yielding my will to His.

Having a mentor like Jesus Christ comes with an awakening of the spirit man that lives inside you. It involves learning how to have the eyes to see and the ears to hear what your mentor is telling you. Often, it goes against everything you have come to know or been taught in this world. That is usually how a maverick unglues you to elevate your thinking.

Over time, my Maverick Mentor taught me that **the side of you that wins the battle is not just the one that is awakened, it is the one that you are feeding the most.** That is **lesson one** of Mentored by a Maverick.

Round Up Questions:

1.) What 'Pappyisms" or other words of wisdom have you heard in your life?

2.) Describe any close calls you have had with death. How have you equated them with a spiritual battle for your life? How has it made you squeeze more out of life?

3.) Has the spiritual dog in you been awakened? (Have you ever asked Jesus Christ to be your personal Lord and Savior?) Are you on His team or still trying Him to get on yours? What is the difference to you?

4.) Describe your quiet place where you talk to God.

5.) What kind of food are you feeding each dog? Which dog is being fed the most? Which dog is winning the fight? If that is not the outcome you want, how are you going to change it?

CHAPTER 3

"Finding the Best Way"

A wound to the chest can be fatal. That's why ancient warriors wore a chest plate to cover their heart and lungs. It was often made of leather or heavy linen or pieces of metal hammered to fit the wearer. All the western cowboy had to protect his chest was his fringed cowhide leather jacket or leather "duster" which was a bit longer.

In "Once Upon A Time In The West" another of my favorite cowboy characters appears. In the opening scene, gunmen wearing dusters approach a solitary train depot. When the train finally arrives, a nameless harmonica-playing stranger (Charles Bronson) starts a tension-filled conversation with the three men in dusters. In the ensuing showdown shootout, all four men end up flat in the dirt. Only the man with the harmonica gets up again.

In the following scene, during a wedding feast

21

preparation on a remote farm called Sweetwater, a group of five gunmen in duster overcoats appear and kill everyone in sight.

Cutting to another dramatic moment in the dark corner of the town tavern, the harmonica player softly blows a tune. A bully named Cheyenne dubs him "Harmonica." Noticing the ringleader is wearing a duster like the previous gunmen, Harmonica starts a conversation:

Harmonica: "I saw three of these dusters a short time ago. They were waiting for a train. Inside the dusters, there were three men."

Cheyenne: "So?"

Harmonica: "Inside the men, there were three bullets."

Cheyenne: "That's a crazy story, Harmonica, for two reasons. One, nobody around these part's got the guts to wear those dusters except Cheyenne's men. Two, Cheyenne's men don't get killed."

Harmonica: "Well, you know music, and you can count."

[*Cheyenne menacingly spins the magazine of his revolver*]

Cheyenne: "All the way up to six if I have to..."

Cheyenne is annoyed that rivals may be copying his trademark dusters to pin killings on his gang. His men's duster jackets and Harmonica's trademark fringed jacket set them apart from the normal townspeople. It brands them just like righteousness brands a believer. (Not self-righteousness, which is not righteous at all but the sin of pride). This righteousness which brands a believer is a moment by moment obedience to the Word of God.

But like the outlaw he is, Satan most fiercely attacks the believers inner man, within their emotions and thought. Without that righteous duster, he seeks to pummel our heart and soul. To mislead and confuse us, he clouds our minds with false truth and puts doubt into the truth of God's Word. He uses the instances of our past to steal the seed of revelation God places in our heart.

We need a heart shield, a spiritual fringed jacket or duster. Having the covering for our heart out of sturdy material is important because God shares Himself in heart to hearts with believers. He gives us what He has, even His only Son, that we might have the power to resist the enemy's schemes. It allows us to know who we are in Christ and that we have everything we need.

The Son of God Himself used this chest shield to prevent a heart "attack." There was one time He was sleeping on a boat and everyone around Him was panicking during a storm. Waking Him urgently, they tried to rile Him also, but He stayed calm and secure. Secure in His righteousness, He calmed the storm. His heart was secure. He was not deceived in His emotions or thoughts.

Another time, He approached a demon possessed man in the caves out of town. His righteousness made Him unafraid and willing to be obedient to minister to the man in spite of apparent dangers. I wanted this kind of righteousness that my maverick mentor displayed. He knew what I hadn't yet learned, 'God's way is always better than my own way.'

Since I was a pretty "wise in my own eyes" guy, it would take some convincing that ANYONE's way was better than mine. As that spirit man in me awakened, I knew training in the art of righteousness needed to take place. The mind and the emotions were two areas where Satan most fiercely attacked. How tightly could I wrap that jacket around my heart before my emotions got the best of me and I went out of my mind?

My first test came on a golf course in Paradise Valley, Arizona.

Monsoon Season

If you know Arizona, then you know about monsoon season. The days are long, hot and humid. The cloudless, signature blue skies give way to massive dust storms with high winds blowing in heavy dark clouds releasing downpours that last through the night. The next morning brings a clear perfectly blue sky and it stays that way until the dust storms return late in the day. It's like nature resets itself – the day is born again. A "do-over" I say out loud as I chuckle to myself. I wish it were that simple.

Time to build myself up with my pre-work pep talk. "I'm Rob and I'm a custom builder. Today, I'm starting a publicity project for a celebrity client. The sun is high in the sky. My crew is here and ready to get started. It's a big house, 10,000 square feet and I am going to build the incredible from the impossible!"

I have reviewed the plans to add a magnificent second level to the house. It included a lavish lovers retreat for the owners, complete with a picturesque view of the 9th hole of a Paradise Valley golf course.

As a builder you would typically avoid opening up roofs during the monsoon season, but it doesn't deter me. As a third generation builder, Mother Nature and I are old adversaries. I can build anything and I know I can make this happen. I've done my homework. The weather reports said the monsoons are good eight days out. My thinking is, "With a big enough crew, I can get this job done fast!" It's a gutsy move, but that's me – I know the game, I've got it covered. My twelve-man crew got started and by 3pm on the first day, we'd torn the whole roof off. Cockily, we left only the rafters. The ceiling joists and the sheet rock from the first floor were exposed. I have pushed my men to their limits and all has gone according to my plan. The hot sun was shining brightly as we secured the tools and called it a day - job well done. I left the job site in good spirits.

That night I took my bride out to a romantic dinner; the best that money could buy. We had much to celebrate. We were young, in love, and making some serious money! We toasted each other in our good fortune and to the bright future ahead. We left the restaurant around 9 pm. We were on our way home when it started to rain. My thoughts immediately turned toward the job. I knew as the man in charge that I had to go back. Even though my men had secured the jobsite well, we did not cover the open roof with plastic. I had a sick feeling in the pit of my stomach as we approached the golf course drive.

By the time we arrived, it was raining so hard my wife stayed dry in the truck while I ran toward the house. Inwardly I was freaking out – obviously, the weather reports had been wrong. The client met me at the front door with fire in her eyes. Immediately upon entering, I could see water pouring through the light fixtures and sparking. I stood rooted to one spot as if lightning itself had struck me there. I could see water dripping off the chandeliers onto expensive carpet. As I moved through the house, the client followed me. Her yelling was a distant faint chirping as my brain buzzed, whirring to calculate the cost of damages that were both seen and unseen. My chest was heaving, but it wasn't from the pace.

Heavy hearted, I climbed up into the attic to look

above the ceiling. Just as I had suspected, the wind had played havoc with the puffy insulation pulling it completely out in some places leaving only the soggy sheet rock and piles of rain-soaked pink mush in others. I could see water standing between the ceiling joists under the rafters, probably throughout the entire attic. The open roof was like a giant dish of water that some mutt was slurping. My mind crashed – what do I do first? The storm continued full-on outside and the one inside me raged. While I was surveying thousands of dollars of potential damage, the client screamed up at me that even her furs in her fur closet were getting wet. I could only numbly respond, "Can't you move them?" – I did not wait for a reply.

Be it pride, desperation or both, the need to control the situation came over me. With the heavens open over both the golf course and the skeletal roofing structure beside me, I thought. "This is ironic; one side is dying for rainwater and the other is gonna be dead because of it." How ridiculous I must have looked to my bride as I climbed up the outside ladder and started to bale water off the open roof with a Slurpee cup. It was futile, like saving the Titanic one teaspoon at a time. My heart was pumping hard; my chest was burning as if my soul was on fire. I felt the deep waves of defeat. There was no way for me to fix this fast enough. It was time to go into problem solving mode, my forte. I'm the man. The man in charge.

After securing things on the roof as best as the circumstances would allow, I climbed down to deal with my extremely irate client. I tried to work my magic by offering to put my clients up in a very nice hotel. She adamantly declined and then struck back with "I'm going to sue your *@#." The single resounding thought in my head was, "I'm not even insured."

After a long heated discussion with no resolution, I got

back in the truck where my beautiful, calm wife waited.
I didn't have the heart to tell her they were going to sue us and take everything – we'd lose everything we owned. As I stumbled to get the words out to explain the predicament we were now immersed in, I'll never forget the look in her clear blue eyes as she said, "Let. Go. And. Let. God." How ridiculous I thought. She had absolutely no clue when it came to construction complications. Neither did God. He was in the church business, not construction. Why would He help me with this? This was my problem, not His.

Sitting in the truck, looking in my wife's eyes and hearing her say "Let. Go. And. Let. God." I knew in my heart I didn't receive it. The reason I didn't receive it was because I was sure she had no clue how bad it was, nor did she realize we were going to lose everything because we were going to be sued. With no insurance, I was going to have to suck it up and pay the price. Let go and let God? It was hard to breathe, let alone to just let go.

We drove home that night in silence. Later as I stood by the window in my own house watching the rain come down, I cried out to heaven. While calculating both the client's losses and my own impending financial doom, the pain of futilely bailing water in the driving rain came back. It was useless. I cried my eyes out in the dark. Was anyone listening?

Paradise Valley saw record rainfall that night.

I've always looked older than I am. Consequently, I've always had role models that were a lot more mature than what I really was. Being a third-generation builder, I started out doing construction at the early age of thirteen. I knew how to do EVERYTHING. So with ten years experience, I was one of the youngest men to become a licensed General Contractor at

age 23. I was doing a 45 or 50-year old man's job. My golf
course client probably thought I was in my mid-
30's. She didn't know she had given this job to a 24-year old
with a lot of swagger. Had she known, she never would have
taken a chance on me. She also didn't know I didn't carry any
liability insurance. Although I was heavy on experience, it was
the bravado of youth that I chose to rely on when making
decisions. I figured I didn't really need insurance because
I wasn't going to have an issue.

I KNOW everything – I'M THE MAN!

I'm being real now, because this is who I was before
Christ. I was a new believer on the edge, still operating as "I'm
my own Man."   Although my wife and I were newly saved, we
were still not in the position of trusting.

Righteousness? The only righteousness I knew at that
time was self-righteousness. It did not protect my heart at all. I
could feel the heaviness in my chest as I cried out, "Lord, please
help me. I am in over my head here." It was time for me to turn
this job over to Him, for He could do far more with it than I ever
could. But it was only my wife who saw that. Maybe she didn't
know construction but she was getting pretty wise in the Word of
God. She encouraged me again to trust God and let it go. She
gave me this little verse from Proverbs 3:5.

*"Trust in the Lord with all your heart and lean not on
your own understanding. In all your ways, submit to Him and
He will make your paths straight. Do not be wise in your own
eyes, fear the Lord and turn away from evil. It will be healing
to your flesh and refreshment to your bones."*
Proverbs 3:5

I had no other option but to trust God, but it was still
difficult to clue in to that it was ALL I could do.   In my mind, I

was still trying to find a way. I went to sleep that night with the idea that I would get up the next morning, roll up my sleeves and get to work. Again I heard my wife's words, "Let go and let God. He has a way of doing things that you can't." I could only pray. At least now I finally didn't want to be the one in charge. I was willing to let someone else take the heat for this mess.

The next morning about 4:30am or "O'Dark-thirty" as my bride liked to call it, I looked out the window and saw the sky filled with puffy black storm clouds as far as the eye could see. The sick feeling returned to the pit of my stomach.

Wait! Off in the distance, amidst the thunderheads I saw a tiny dot of blue sky. Well, the job site was in the distance too and it was in that same direction....wouldn't it be cool if that was over my job? As I drove there, I had the hope that the blue spot of sky would get bigger, and it did. Each mile closer to the job was lifting my spirits as the sun shone brighter and brighter.

Surveying the job in the light of day, the damage did not seem as drastic as the night before. The hot Arizona sun was drying things out just as it always did. The roof seemed to be drying with minimal damage. Although my client rode my rear all day with threats and insults, I worked the crew hard all day, again pushing my men to the limits. I needed to redeem myself by finishing this job at a record pace with no more monsoon damage. I could not wait to be done with this project. At the end of the day, I made my crew meticulously drape plastic sheeting over the roof to try protect the ceilings, carefully tucking and screwing it securely into place in preparation for that night's monsoon winds and rain. I had done the best that I could. But ultimately, it wasn't up to me. I wasn't in charge anymore.

Record rains were recorded in Paradise Valley for the

second night in a row and I woke suspecting the worst. I forced myself to stay home and pray instead of beating myself up at the job and worrying about what could happen. But again the next morning, I walked outside to see the thickly clouded dark sky and there in the distance, the tiniest patch of blue. My hope rose up in a giddy laughter. Could my job be supernaturally protected?

When I arrived at the job site, the wind had pulled off all the plastic sheeting in the night and had again blown it out onto the golf course. I about had a heart attack right in the cab of my pickup. "Judgment time," I thought. I have to go up on that roof and assess the destruction.

To my surprise, there was zero water damage. It was like a little inside joke. The wind had powerfully ripped off the covering that I had arranged to protect the job. God was showing me that plastic was nothing compared to the covering He could place on the project. Still, I went to work like mad, pretending my effort mattered. I pushed my crew hard that whole day and again we draped plastic over the site for the night. Again, for the third night, record rains.

The following sunrise, God dazzled me again. It wasn't until that day, that I fully realized that every single day, I was beckoned on my morning drive by a clear spot of blue sky over the house. Through this, it was driving me to my knees but I had never stopped worrying. I was never confident enough to say, "God's got this." Every single day I'd show my lack of faith by buttoning down the hatches as best I could in case it rained. I expected it to rain. I was surprised by God's faithfulness.

I'd get up in the morning, go outside and look. Way off in the distance would be the same little blue spot. It was amazing! It was then that it clicked in my brain: "My plastic wasn't protecting my job. God was." It was at that moment I truly Let. Go. And. Let. God. As a new believer, I was amazed that He would do this for me. I fell to my knees and wept. He really did have my back.

The next morning, my irate client called to complain that it was raining on the driveway, raining on the front lawn, and hailing on the golf course behind, but not over her house. Somehow, that made her even angrier than ever. I was grateful beyond belief.

"What's going on?" she shouted. I told her it was God. She said it was strange and she didn't believe in that stuff, but she could not deny the fact that every day it wasn't raining over her house, but it was in her backyard and on the street out front.

Like a promise kept, the clear blue patch of sky appeared day after day. I was incredulous every day, almost singing "He did it again and again, and again." Even though it was there the day before, the next day it was a new and amazing thing He did. That's why it's such a humongous thing to happen one day, but it happened day after day.

On the eighth day, when the exterior of the house was complete, it finally rained like crazy on the house. The windows of heaven opened. Paradise Valley had even more record rains that week and there were literally no leaks in the house. It was an amazing example of God's hand, His protection. There was no interior damage. The ceilings did not fall in. It had dried-in to perfection, no discoloration in the drywall, no bowing in the sheetrock. The blown fiberglass insulation in the attic that was once wet and soggy, dried puffy. Even the clients' furs dried perfectly. **It was miraculous!**

My gratitude was so great that the emotion of it would

often break me down to my knees sobbing. I told the story to anyone that came through the construction site. The crew would say this was the most amazing house they've ever worked on. What resonated with me was that HE would do this for me! God had to bring me something so big that even in my own power could not solve it. I had to get to my knees to trust Him. And I finally got it. His righteousness was at stake and He took it seriously. Would I? Would I trust that God had a way of doing things that was so far above my thinking that He would mentor me?

At the end of the job, I prayed to God and thanked Him. I felt like He asked me, "Why do you wait until you have a problem to ask for my help? Why don't you ask for my help before you start? You and I are partners, Pardner!"

Years and countless projects have passed since that time God helped me. I've learned that my success is not me, it is all God working through me. I have no ability, it's all His ability. Finally, I learned to put Him first and realize that His way is the best way.

It doesn't take a storm now to make me draw my duster closer and trust God and His way of doing things. But my duster has some awesome fringe on it that helps protect me too.

Fringe

When I was young and naive, I had no idea of battles I was about to undertake as a believer in Christ. My mentor cowboy taught me that no war should be entered into without a covering to protect one's vital organs. The cowboy jacket often had a special feature: Fringe. The fringe on a cowboy's jacket was often thought to be a decorative touch.

Fringe served several purposes. By cutting the excess jacket material into strips, it also allowed the cowboy to pull off a piece of fringe to tie something in an emergency. In a pinch, cutting off a strip of fringe would provide a string that was just right for re-attaching reins to a bit, or replacing a string on a saddle. Whether it was lashing together an emergency shelter or lashing the end of a rope to keep it from fraying, those strips of leather came in real handy at awkward times.

If that wasn't enough, fringe actually served another distinct and practical purpose. Since water tended to run in rivulets downward off the body, the addition of fringe directed the damaging water away from body of the coat. Acting as tiny wicks to disperse water, fringe allowed the garment to shed rain and to dry faster.

My maverick showed me the need for this flexible body shield which had extra material to wick away danger. He taught me to seek righteousness - the power to do things God's way and a belief that God's way is better than my own. My spiritual fringed jacket would help shed the selfish thinking that I always had the best way and would also wick away the views of the world so I wouldn't become soaked. It also provided me some extra pieces to help me mend together some brokenness in others.

Just like a kid running out the door without a coat when it was freezing outside, it took some time for me to listen to my mentor about taking my jacket. Immaturity can make one hardheaded and my mind was tough to change. Would God's way really be the best way? It was most evident when God taught me the best car buying secret of all time.

Best Car Buying Secret of All Time

Like most any guy I love cars. I mean, I really love cars! For me, they aren't just transportation, they are a business investment. I buy and sell cars for a hobby like some guys play golf. The difference between golf and car-buying is that I almost always make a profit. Sniffing out car deals is a skill I learned from my father. (My mother says it is more like a "sickness"). His instinct for finding a killer deal on a great car was like magic.

As my father before me, I have owned over 70 cars so far in my life. I like the way they look, the way they sound and the art of making a deal. As a result, I don't really ever get attached to any particular car. Once I even had someone offer me cash for my car while I was working a construction job. Not surprisingly, I called my bride to pick me up at the end of the day because I was car-less (but my wallet was full).

This particular time, I had come across a really sweet deal on a fairly new Jaguar convertible at an exotic car dealership in Kaka'ako on Oahu in Hawaii. If there is good deal to be found, I will find it. And there it was. Parked in the center of the showroom floor was this car. It was a symbol of European excellence, titanium-colored with a black canvas convertible top. It reeked of sleekness and elegance starting from the iconic leaping cat on the hood all the way back to the taillights. I thought to myself, "YEAH, I've got to have that!" I jumped in to the luxurious leather seats and took off for a test drive.

The smooth power of 12-cylinders spoke to me. It said, "Take me home, Rob, I'm yours." Even as I drove back to the dealership, I had already calculated a win/win deal in my head to buy the car. Soon, I was seated with the owner of the dealership and the deal was worked out. I would bring the cash back the next day and he wanted me to take the car home for the night. (Partly because it was the end of the month and partly because he wanted me to fall so in love with the car that I wouldn't talk myself out of the deal.) Elated, I took the keys and I left with the exquisite driving machine. I meandered home with the top down and marveled at its beauty and handling. After I got home and everyone in the family had their turn for a ride, I just stood in the driveway and stared at this beautiful Jaguar. Like I said, I have bought dozens of cars, but this one was really something special.

Just then, I felt as though the Lord spoke to me and said, "You know, you never really asked me about this car before you decided to buy it." Sure enough, that was true. I felt kind of convicted, but not enough to do anything about it. It was a REALLY nice car and I REALLY wanted it. I should have remembered that my God has a particular way of doing things. His way is always the best way. And it is always for my benefit.

Later that night, before going to bed, I was saying my

evening prayers and decided I wanted to go to sleep with a clear conscience. Cautiously, I prayed to God saying, "Okay, this is the deal: If I've done wrong and I'm not supposed to have this car, God, please don't let me sleep." (I often pray prayers like this and although I never regret the lessons, I suppose I really should think it through first before I pray those kinds of prayers). I was really tired and fell into bed dreaming of driving that car on date nights with my bride as we zoomed along the beaches of Hawaii.

You guessed it. Midnight...still awake. 1 a.m....tossing and turning. 2 a.m....wondering how I am going to function all day tomorrow on the job with no rest. This was getting ridiculous.

Finally, at 3 a.m. I found myself outside, standing on my driveway staring at the car. "Okay God, I get it. I'm supposed to give it back." That was piercing. I had never gone back on a deal. How would this play out? My flesh conjured up reasons why I shouldn't do this. I sincerely struggled with the integrity issue. How was it going to look for me to take it back and tell them I've changed my mind? Maybe the dealership owner wouldn't let me out of the agreement? "Could I keep it then, God?" After more thought and prayer I decided I would take it back, but of course, I negotiated a new deal....with GOD. Here was my counteroffer: "Okay God, when I take this fine Jag back to the dealership, if the owner gives me anything besides "okay", I will just go ahead, follow through and buy the car because you raised me to be a man of my word."

Doesn't that sound like a reasonable plan? On the one hand, I felt pretty certain that if I were the dealership owner, I would raise an objection. In reality, I had pretty much convinced myself it was going to go my way. Since I am a pretty good judge of human behavior, I determined that I would probably end up with the car. I went inside the house and fell into a fitful sleep.

The next day, I had all day to drive the car, look at the car, mess with the car and play with the car... I LOOOOOOVED THE CAR! So after work, I went to the dealership and walked into the owner's office. From behind his desk, he rose to shake my hand and greeted me with a "Good afternoon, Mr. Moore." Ready to face God's request to "try" and return the car, I sat down across from him, took the keys out and laid them on his desk. Trying to be blunt and get a reaction, I said, "I don't want your car." There I said it. I stood ready for his objection so that I could recant and go ahead and buy the car to appease him. Surely, he would take my comment as a hurdle to overcome but find a way to convince me to take it.

Strangely, he looked at me, reached over and picked up the keys and said, "Okay." He dropped the keys back in his lap drawer and nodded goodbye to me as he went back to his paperwork. "That's it? I'm dismissed without even a word. What?" I was so ready for the fight that I was let down that all he said was "okay." It was done. No car. God had the final word. Car #53 was given back to the dealership. Oh yeah, to add to the humble pie, I was now car-less in downtown Kaka'ako. I was forced to take the city **bus** back to the house. Did I mention that I am a car guy? I had never been on the bus. What a long trip that turned out to be as God spoke to me all the way home.

Realizing the thing is not about the thing, I asked myself, "What was the real issue here?" The issue was that God wants to be a part of every decision in my life. His righteousness doesn't care about my car, my deals or my ride. He cares about having every piece of my heart. Was I disappointed? No, because He is who He is, I came out better than I was before. He wants to know that I put Him above all else in my life. Even my ride.

Especially my ride. Since then, he has said, "Yes!" to several Jaguars. But more importantly, I have learned to ask him FIRST before I venture out to make a deal. When He goes before me, I need never be turned back again. Now that I have learned the lesson to let Him lead, He puts me in the right place at the right time. That's the best car buying secret of all time. When I righteously honor God, He makes more out of my life than I could ever imagine. God's way (righteousness) is really the best business investment that I could ever make.

In the same way, righteousness covers and protects the believer from heart damage. My heart is susceptible to the wickedness and negativity of this world. If I take away all the choices that are NOT God's way of doing things, the remaining choices become pretty clear. When Jesus died on the cross, His righteousness was credited to all who believe in Him. It keeps my heart strong and pure for God. It reminds me that God has a better way for us, even when we don't understand. I need to be smarter than the enemy and protect my heart. It reminds me of one of my favorite westerns, "A Fistful of Dollars".

A Man with No Name (Clint Eastwood), arrives at a little Mexican border town. He spies an opportunity to make a "fistful of dollars." He ends up in a shootout, a duel to the death, with the evil Ramon from the Rojos gang. The Man with No Name has a steel chest plate hidden under his clothing and advises Ramon to "aim for the heart." Of course, the bullets bounce off, Clint wins the battle and rides off into the sunset. Just as A Man With No Name protected his heart from attack, I need to do the same in the spiritual realm or the enemy will get the best of my mind and emotions.

This isn't just in my job of construction work or hobby of purchasing cars. It included every area of my life, even my physical health. That was to be the biggest test of my life. Could

I really trust that God's way would be the best way or would it break my heart?

Embrace Your Process

Back in 1995, my life consisted of being an avid golfer, long distance runner, scuba diver with instructor certification, surfer, boogie boarder, downhill snow skier, competitive water skier and more. As a true "type A" personality, I loved recharging by heading to the outdoors for physical conditioning. I had been married 10 years, had two (of the soon to be four) kids we would have in our family, and loving my life in Hawaii. One of my passions was running long distance. At that time, I was training for the Honolulu Marathon. I was an active man of God. So, why is it that now I don't I have use of my legs? My diagnosis started with a doctor's visit.

I mentioned to my physician that I had noticed my right running shoe was quite a bit dustier than my left one. It seemed as though I was dragging the ground with my right foot. I thought my running gait might be off due to any number of factors. Curiously, he diagnosed a "foot drop" and recommended that I see a neurologist for further testing. I wasn't expecting that. After an MRI scan of my brain and spine, a number of demyelinated areas showed up across by brain. The unraveled areas resembled frayed electrical cords with wires shorting out. My brain was no longer talking correctly to my feet to tell them to lift and flex. The unhappy diagnosis was eventually multiple sclerosis. I was shocked. I felt great, was in my prime, and engaged in a lot of physical activity. All I could think to say to the doctor was, "I am training for the marathon." He replied, "Don't stop." I didn't. When I cried out to my mentor about it, Jesus said, "Follow me. My way is the best for you." Numbly, I put on my fringed jacket and followed.

The years went by. The disabling symptoms increased as I served the Lord. My balance slowly faded and my leg strength and control weakened. Gradually, I went from an ankle/foot brace, to a knee brace, leg brace, to a walking staff, to a walker (after knee surgery), and finally to an electric cart. I did it all to remain mobile. I refused to stop. It was the maverick in me. When I would cry out in confusion, my mentor again repeated, "Follow me and be faithful." My fringed jacket covered me. He kept me from feeling wounded and shielded my heart.

As my commitment to serve the Lord grew, so did my disabilities. Finally, my speech began to slur, my fine motor skills made it difficult to use my hands, and I got fatigued easily. Some days, it didn't seem fair. Some days it felt like hell, like I was losing my very life that I loved. I've heard it said, "If you find that you're going through hell, don't stop. Keep going forward so that you GET THROUGH IT." I pulled my jacket tighter and kept going. I decided to be "tougher than hell." I am a maverick.

I decided to grow through what I was going through. God had given me a beautiful life partner, my bride, for the journey to keep me company. She was my cheerleader, my encouragement in the tough days. We poured out more ministry days in our latter life by being teachable, available and faithful. We looked at what we were able to do, not what we could no longer accomplish. We found the best in situations, even when the world wanted us to see the worst.

I became limited to this annoying little motorized cart to carry my lifeless legs around but I didn't let that stop me. Even when I took a tumble at the gym (yes, I would still be at the gym working out my upper body), and broke my ankle in two places, it didn't stop me.

My selfless bride turned it into a joy to have my hair washed every morning in the sink shampoo bowl because I couldn't get into the shower with my ankle boot. She was always believing and seeing the best of every situation, but it was my fringed jacket that was my comfort and heart protection from the Lord. It kept me from giving up hope.

Some people believe the old adage, "God won't give you any more than you can handle." I can't find that anywhere in the Bible. If I could always handle everything He gave me, I would never need Him at all. I would have remained wise in my own eyes. I think my God specialized in giving me more than I could handle, because until I got to the end of myself, I never truly needed God. He promised not to tempt me beyond what I can bear without giving me a door of escape (I Corinthians 10:13). He promised never to leave me or forget me (Hebrews 13:5). He always wants me to remain dependent on Him, not leaning on my own understanding (Proverbs 3:5,6). I am grateful that He constantly gives me more than I can handle because it keeps me returning to Him for more and more.

It is explained perfectly in Hebrews 12 (MSG) "In this all-out match against sin, others have suffered far worse than you, to say nothing what Jesus went through - all that bloodshed! So don't feel sorry for yourselves... God is educating you; that's why you must **never** drop out. He's treating you as dear children. This trouble you're in isn't punishment; it's *training*...so why not embrace God's training so we can truly live? ...God is doing what is best for us, training us to live God's Holy best. At the time, discipline isn't much fun. It always feels like it's going against the grain. Later, of course, it pays off handsomely, for it's the well-trained who find themselves mature in their relationship with God." Amen. I have learned God's way is better than my way.

I now truly understand that my "process" is not about me, but completely about Him. His righteousness or way of doing things is all I am interested in. With my disabilities, I truly have reached more people's hearts than I ever did in my own strength. In my weakness, Jesus Christ really has been made strong.

In teaching me about the value of my cowhide jacket, I learned a great and powerful lesson from my Maverick Mentor. **No matter what happens, I won't stop believing that God's way is the best way.** That's **lesson two**, pardner.

Round Up Questions:

1.) Do you have anything you wear that sets you apart from everyone else? Is there anyone else's way that you consistently consider as better than your own?

2.) What does righteousness mean to you? Can you give an example of righteousness that you have seen?

3.) What area do you love, know or have authority over that makes you difficult to be led by anyone else? Describe a time when God's way turned out to be the best way.

4.) How has the enemy crept into your chest shield and attacked your heart? What training have you been experiencing?

5.) What can you do to more effectively shield your heart and other vital organs from damage?

ROB and ROBIN MOORE

CHAPTER 4

"Buckle Up or Buckle Under"

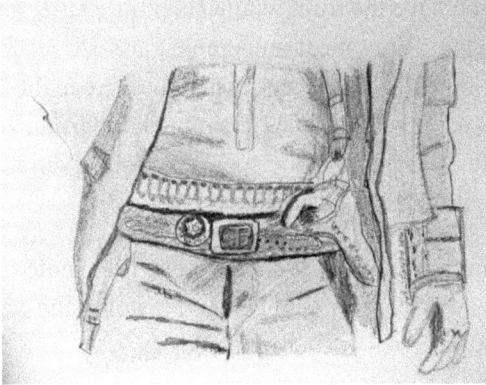

Truth Trumps Reality

In the movie from the "Dollars Trilogy" *For a Few Dollars More*, Clint Eastwood (the Man With No Name) is an impressive shot. The skill with which he draws his gun from his gun belt is legendary. After he and the bounty hunter, Mortimer, escaped the outlaw gang, Clint has the evil ringleader, El Indio, covered with a rifle. Not just any rifle, but an 1854 Jennings Rifle Company Volcanic Rifle.

And how did I know that? Me and every other kid in my neighborhood could list all the Hollywood cowboys (including the names of their horses) and could definitely tell which cowboy was which just by looking at his six guns and holsters. *The "Walk and Draw" or "Spaghetti Western"* gun holster design came into being in the late 1950's. This rig became even more popular in movies such as "The Good, Bad, and the Ugly", "A Fistful of Dollars".....all of the classics with Clint

Eastwood. This became the gun belt of choice in all the television and movie westerns.

In the natural, a gun belt holds your weapon and your ammunition. In the supernatural, it surrounds your most vulnerable parts and holds up your spiritual pants. Truth is the same way. When you have the truth, you walk a little taller and feel a little more secure. Your most vulnerable parts are secured in the truth and you don't have to worry about getting caught with your pants down. When you stand firm upon the truth, you become unshakeable. Everything God speaks is truth, even if it doesn't yet line up with what we can see.

Back to Clint Eastwood. He forces the evil El Indio to wait while he gives away his own gun belt and pistol to the bounty hunter, Mortimer, which evens the odds.

"Now we start," the Man With No Name announces, and sits down while Mortimer and El Indio pace off for a showdown. The music finishes, and Mortimer outdraws and guns down El Indio. The Man With No Name retrieves his gun belt and rounds up the bad guys bodies to collect his bounty. Why did Clint give up his gun belt? He knows that he has nothing to worry about. Mortimer is on his side. And, he still holds the rifle. The Man With No Name is confident in the outcome. He knows the truth (what you can't always see) and the truth trumps reality (what you do see.)

Deception is one of the Enemy's oldest tactics, but my maverick mentor told me that "I am the way and the truth and the life. No one comes to the Father except through me." (John 14:6, NIV) Who was I going to be listening to for my wisdom? Would I be rattled by the voices in my head pointing out my reality or would I be like Clint and rely on God's truth? Some hired hands think that truth is what you can see and they can't

wait to tell you the "truth" about yourself. My Maverick Mentor
has taught me that the truth is what HE says, and it is not always
what you can see. Some times you just need to stand firm in
knowing the truth. It trumps reality every time.

There was a time when my bride and I were young
Christians and we thought we had everyone fooled. We were
keeping a secret, but God knew the truth. My mentor was on our
side.

Secrets Couples Keep

Have you ever come across a photo album or some
pictures laying around when you had decided, "I'm going to
straighten up in here and get organized?" Do you open the
album and thumb through the pictures or do you keep working?
Of course you open it! It's fun to see pictures of how things used
to be. Perhaps it's your old hairstyle or a goofy outfit that you
want to keep a secret. Perhaps there are more things from your
past that you haven't wanted anyone to know. Today, I'd like to
share a story that I see in the picture book of my mind; one
where I see my growth and how you can't keep a secret from
God.

Many years ago my young bride and I were youth
leaders at a church in Phoenix, AZ. This was during the time we
were the "Joneses" with the big house, the swimming pool, and
both drove Corvettes. We were young in our walk with God
and very eager to figure things out. We certainly made a few
mistakes along the way. Construction work had run low and we
wound up living on credit cards for a time. In order to eat, we
had resorted to selected restaurants we knew would run the credit
card transactions "manually" – old school style. You might
remember the days when they laid your plastic card on top of a
little metal grater and placed a carbon slip on top of it. Sliding a

plate across the top, it made an imprint of your credit card on the carbon-lined paper. The server would then fill in the transaction amount by hand before returning it for the tip. Back in those days, not every business was able to swipe your card. If our card had the misfortune to be run electronically, we knew it would be rejected because we were way over our limits and living on the edge. We were good at keeping the secret that we were failing financially.

During this lean time in our lives, our joy was in our church youth group. The truth wasn't always what you could see, but we needed to speak the truth so we can see what we were saying. Truthfulness was in short supply. Truth said we were like trees planted by rivers of living water and what ever we did would prosper (Jeremiah 17:8 & Psalm 1:1-3). Reality said we were broke. Truth said we would reap with the same measure of generosity that we sowed (Luke 6:38 & 2 Corinthians 9:6-8). Reality was that we were sowing like crazy and nothing was sprouting up. Truth said that the Lord is the one who gave us the ability to produce wealth (Deuteronomy 8:18), but Reality was that we had created a lot of debt. Truth said our Lord owns the cattle on a thousand hills. Reality is that we really needed a cow. Unless you have the Truth firmly girded about your soft underbelly, it is easy for Reality to be what you stand upon. There were days as a young husband that I wondered if I would be able to take care of my wife, much less the kids we might have one day. I knew the Truth of God, but all the Truth in the world is meaningless unless you put it under your standing. I remember my wife reminding me over and over again, "If you don't stand firm in your faith, you will not stand at all. (Isaiah 7:9) It was time for me to buckle up, not buckle under.

Truth, the Word of God, was the only thing we really had to stand firm on. We led our group to do crazy things like: have an Acts 19:19 party (more about that later), or go feed migrant farm workers in the corn fields at night (John 21:15-17), or spend an entire day in prayer and fasting (Matthew 6:16-18).

This prayer and fasting day - all 24 hours of it, had about 30 kids participating. We gathered at sundown Friday night to begin the fast at the church. Competitive and excited, we spent the evening doing group team building games and hanging out (but no food!). About 10pm, we split the group. Boys came with me to spend the night at our house. The girls spent the night with my wife at the church. The next morning, we all reunited at our house for a whole day of fasting and praying; gathering on the hour every hour until sundown. It was our time to seek and be completely with our Lord.

There came a time when it was noticed by the kids that we didn't have anything in our refrigerator except a gallon jug of water and some condiments. My wife and I knew it was empty because we were broke. We didn't have any money to stock the fridge, but the kids thought we took everything out of the refrigerator so they wouldn't be tempted. "You guys are so INCREDIBLE!" they said with laughing amazement in their voices. My wife and I just smiled widely and said "Yeah, that's right!" We avoided looking at each other.

That evening, the group decided to break the fast at the local pizza joint. To honor their youth pastors, the kids insisted on pitching in together to pay for our meal. We humbly accepted with gratitude (this was one of those places that swiped your credit card). As we broke our fast and celebrated together at the pizza buffet, we all had plenty to eat.

The picture in the photo album of my mind is a picture of an answered prayer: one hungry couple and a group of teens that blessed them beyond measure by buying their meal. We had no idea that God was just getting started.

Before leaving that night, we stood together and prayed over the kids and as each went their own way. Feeling light-hearted, my bride and I talked happily all the way home about the experience we'd just had.

As we walked up to the house, we saw an envelope taped to the glass on our front door. Quickly deflating, our first emotion was dread. Was it a bill collector leaving a notice on the door? Was our house being foreclosed upon? We hesitantly approached the walkway. Who would be leaving something on our door on a weekend at this hour?

Reaching out, I pulled the envelope from the door and realized there were actually two of them taped together. Something was scrawled on the outside but it was too dark to read. I had forgotten to leave the porch light on and the glow from the streetlight was to dim to make out the words. Unlocking the door, I handed my bride one, while I kept the other.

As we entered and sat on the couch, we discovered that written on the front of each envelope was a Scripture reference from the Bible. Eager to find out what was inside, even before we looked up the Scripture verse, we tore open one envelope and then the other. Stunned, we turned over the identical paper inside each one. A $200 gift certificate for the local grocery store was written out and stamped. ($400 total). That was back in the day before plastic gift cards were so common. Baffled beyond belief, we animatedly rushed through a conversation.

"Who gets someone a gift certificate from a GROCERY STORE?"

"Who could have come here while we were gone?"

"Who has that kind of money to throw around?"

We questioned each other to find out if either of us had let on how strapped financially we were to anyone, Nope. No dice. We had kept this secret well.

Because there was Scripture on each of the envelopes, we were pretty sure that neither of our unchurched families had anything to do with it. It couldn't have been one of the youth because most of them were with us. Amazed, we looked at each other and then back at the envelopes. One had Psalm 34:10 scrawled across it and the other had 2 Corinthians 9:12-15.

Those were not familiar Scriptures to either of us. My wife ran for her bible and we eagerly looked them up. My eyes filled with tears as I heard my wife read the first one.

"The lions may grow weak and hungry,
but those who seek the Lord lack no good thing."
Psalm 34:10

Really? Who knew how hungry we were in those days? No one. Well, no one but God. Truth. In those days, our pride would have never allowed us to let anyone know about our financial failure. Reality.

I looked up the second Scripture and I tried not to choke as I read out loud,

"This service that you perform is not only supplying the needs of the Lord's people but is also overflowing in many expressions of thanks to God. Because of the service by which you have proved yourselves, others will praise God for the obedience that accompanies your confession of the gospel of Christ, and for your generosity in sharing with them and with everyone else. And in their prayers for you their hearts will go out to you, because of the surpassing grace God has given you." 2 Corinthians 9:12-15

Thanks be to God for His indescribable gift!

Wow. We felt as though God himself had inscribed those words personally just as a message to us. Nobody, and I mean NOBODY, knew we were lacking – except God. Our precious Father, the great giver of provision had told SOMEBODY. Somebody had blessed us with $400! In order to do this, it meant they had to go against everything they could see and know (Reality).

We thought our secret was safe because we looked like two kids living high on the hog. We were driving Corvettes and appeared to be living large in a four bedroom house with a swimming pool. Certainly, it had to be someone trained to be obedient to the voice of God not what they seemed to see with their own two eyes, someone who leaned on the Truth. Oh! How we wanted to know who that person was.

The next day at church we looked every person in the eye as we greeted them. Not one twinkle. Not one crack of a smile. We tried to linger a bit longer to see if we could identify our mysterious benefactor. Not even one hint of who was responsible. All the while and to this very day, we have no idea who blessed us at one of our greatest times of need, so we just say, "Praise God." And I think our gift certificate benefactor wanted it that way.

So, as I close the picture book in my mind, I'm reminded that I'm a blessed man driven daily to my knees in awe of the love the Father has for us. The last photo my mind sees is a handwritten note to myself that says,

"Things are not always what they seem, but there is One who sees all things." No secrets.

Reality seems real, doesn't it? But the Truth is what we

need to buckle up around us. Through the last twenty years my bride and I (along with several others) have had to choose..."Would we believe the truth to be the reality of what we saw or the reality of what God saw in us?" There are some truths I wish I knew before I became a pastor, but I wasn't ready to hear the truth, much less buckle up with it, but the Maverick Mentor guides us into all truth.

What Pastors Wish

Sometime you don't know WHAT you don't know. Ever wonder what pastors wish they knew? Before I became a pastor, God tried to tell me what I didn't know. I just wasn't ready to listen. Sound familiar? Here is how it happened....

- She gripped my shoulder and began to murmur, then her voice grew louder and more insistent,
- "You, Rob Moore... You are multi-gifted and multi-talented.
- But God wants a focus for you in the awareness that your best years are ahead......."
- Those were the words of prophetess Jean Darnall.

When I was a construction project manager in Hawaii, my boss was the owner of the company. He had hired me from a newspaper ad in Arizona and moved me all the way to Hawaii with my bride after only a few phone conversations. Turned out that we were kindred spirits. Brothers from another mother. Did I mention he was Chinese? Doesn't matter. Mack Mao was a man after God's own heart and I was his right hand man. Interesting thing about Mack was that he wanted more than anything to become a pastor. He was training me to be at the helm of his construction company as he moved into ministry.

On this particular day, Mack took me with him to a

luncheon he was hosting for some pastors from our local denomination. Jean Darnall, the charismatic church planter, evangelist, healer, prophetess was the guest of honor.

Following the lunch, the pastors were asked to remain behind to be prayed over by Jean. I made a beeline for the door but Mack asked me to stay. As this sweet little old lady made her way down the line of pastors, I felt like an imposter in the most intense way. If she was really hearing from God, I would be exposed in just a few minutes for being just a run-of-the-mill regular guy who overstayed his lunch invitation.

My mind was racing and thoughts were bouncing so loud that I barely heard anything she said before she came to me. This kindly sweet-faced woman reached up and planted her hands on my shoulders.

A gift from God to the church, Jean reminded me of a meek, quiet, cookie-baking grandma...until she opened her mouth. That's when I felt the power of God course through my bones from the words she spoke. Her eyes were shut and she began to speak with the presence and authority of a ruler of nations. What came out of her mouth was so powerful and strong. It was so encouraging. It was so specific. Her assistant tried to record much of what she said to me. When she finished, the assistant ripped off the page he had written and stuffed it in my hand as she moved to the pastor next to me.

The scrawl on the page read, "You, Rob Moore... You are multi-gifted and multi-talented. But God wants a focus for you in the awareness that your best years are ahead. Focus all of your energies and skills, as you do so it will expand and spread out. Limited focus is for you at this time. It won't rob you of versatility. It will only deepen your gifts and versatility. I see a channel, a gorge, a flow of life and direction for you. God will give you a forward sense of direction. God has taken hold of you, focus your skills on a goal to meet a particular purpose. God has put you in a church to help you focus. Your ministry will go beyond your church. It will appear for a time that you have lost everything but it shall all be returned to you and more. You are a media person, a multi-media person. God will release a multi-media vanguard ministry that will go many directions and expand throughout the earth. Proceed in God's direction, through your church."

It was not everything I remember she had said to me, but it was powerful nonetheless. I stood silently, eyes closed and talked to God. "God, you know my future. You know the plans you have for me. Plans to not harm me, to give me a future and a hope. I want everything you have for me God. Here I am."

Little did I know that God was about to take my life on a grand detour. A trip across the Pacific Ocean was about to give me some direction.

Fast forward two years. Mack had entered the pastorate and I was leading my own construction company. Specializing in American Disabilities Act (retrofitting for compliance to the law), the company was booming. We were in the middle of building sixty construction companies in sixty cities and we were already operating in five states. This was a major undertaking and I was working with my hair on fire. My walk with Him had matured to the point where I heard Him regularly and each time it was with the ears of a humble and obedient servant. So when He spoke THAT DAY there was no doubt.

Sitting in a Sunday morning church service, my Pastor began talking about planting a church in San Diego. My heart quickened and I very clearly heard God say, "He is talking about you." I instantly discounted myself. No, it can't be me. My construction companies were my profession. Fear welled up in me. My gunbelt had slipped low on my hips. C'mon! I wasn't pastor material. There was no bible college in my history. God was mistaken.

After the service, I wandered around the courtyard. I heard myself say, "Father, can you really be calling me? Do you know my past?"

In the quiet of the outdoors around me, He responded, "I don't remember your past, son. Do YOU know your future?" Wow. That was a new one. For the first time, I didn't know what my future held.

From that point, I felt it was time to move forward with a plan. I wanted to force God's hand to show me what I didn't know. Later that night at dinner, I asked my wife what she thought. She remained neutral, neither encouraging or discouraging.

A wild plan began to form in my head. I would fly to San Diego and fast and pray until God revealed what I was supposed to do. This was extreme, even for a guy like me, so I decided to sleep on it. The next day, on our date night, I approached my wife cautiously about the idea. I would be leaving her with our four small kids and our coffee business to run (as well as any construction emergencies that arose while I was gone). So I needed to have her on board.

To my surprise, she heard me out and replied, "God already told me that you were going. He asked me to keep all influence to myself until you had decided in your heart to make the trip. I already have your suitcase packed. So honey, when are you leaving?"

"What? Are you kidding me?" It seemed like everyone

from my pastor to my wife were in on this but me!

I flew out on Wednesday to San Diego and drove to Del Mar. I planned to fast for 3 days, drinking only water and coffee – So here I was, sitting in a local Starbucks waiting for the grand message from God to tell me what I needed to know. I was praying and said, "God, if I'm on the right journey here, please send somebody to talk to me."

Sure enough, the next person who came in would notice my Bible open and come strike up a conversation. Before long, they would sit down and we would be sharing back and forth.

Later that night, I was sitting at a corner table by myself. It was about 9:30pm and the place was dead. No customers in sight. God and I had this continual conversation going. Here is a typical exchange:

Him: "Move over there and open your Bible."

Me: "Okay, now bring someone to talk to."

Him: "Don't instruct me."

After my little exchange with God, the next person in the door, a man, walked right up to me and said, "Oh, you're reading the Bible, maybe you could help me?" The stranger sat down and began to tell me about the divorce he was going through and the obstacles it had created in his life. I sensed he was desperate for guidance and answers. We talked together for a while and I ministered to him with the Word of God as counsel.

After a time, the man got up to leave. Before he did. he thanked me for talking with him. I couldn't help but grin peacefully as I watched him walk away and I thought how cool that was. I asked God to do it again. God replied, "Don't test me. You asked me to do something and I did it for you."

Sitting with my Bible, I would talk to whoever God brought into my path. One by one, strangers walked up to my table and sat down For the next three days, I listened as they spoke of brokenness of family, health or finances. For some, all they needed was prayer; for others it was holding hands or being in agreement for what God was showing them.

Eagerly, I engaged each person as a potential messenger from God. I wasn't concerned about how I looked or felt; I just wanted someone to tell me that I should be a pastor. No one spoke the words I longed to hear.

Don't get me wrong, I thrived on these discussions about the word and theology and Jesus. But in my fasting, I was more hungry for answers about my own future. Clearly, God had brought me here and had some sort of message for me but I just wasn't getting it.

The three days had passed and it was almost time for my long flight back to Hawaii. It was a beautiful afternoon as I pulled my truck out on to the coastal boulevard to head back to the hotel to pack up. I had the windows rolled all the way down letting in the cool ocean breeze as I drove.   There was a vast, endless ocean on my left and a distant mountain range on my right. Any other time, being surrounded by such God-made natural beauty would inspire a feeling of larger-than-life freedom, but not today.   I felt unfinished and very unsettled. The vibe changed as I entered La Jolla and saw The Cove.

Each day on the drive between my hotel and Starbucks I passed by this beach called "The Cove." Actually, the Cove was just a parking lot and lookout over the ocean. Every time I had driven past the Cove, it would pop in my mind that I should stop there and pray. It was no different as I passed it for the last time.

Again, I felt like God told me that I needed to stop. My excuse this time was that the little parking lot was full. A few minutes later I felt regret as the Spirit chided me.

Unwisely, I started to reason with God – "Couldn't I just go to the beach in Del Mar by the hotel after I check out? It is too hard to turn around in this California highway traffic."

I felt like God said, "I told you to go to the Cove." Sometimes I really don't know that I don't know. Here I was trying to hear the voice of God and when I did, I was arguing with what He was telling me to do. How many times would I be hardheaded? (Don't answer that.) God was trying to gird me with truth but I kept throwing reality back at Him. Eventually, I decided to buckle up.

So, I fought the traffic and I turned around to go back to the Cove...but not without an attitude. Finally, I pulled in to the tiny parking lot which was full. (See God? I told you so.)

Of course, I wanted to get out of the truck and walk up to the Lookout – the views were absolutely flawless. There was no separation between the blue skies and endless blue waters. The cove and beach were tucked between adjacent sandstone cliffs. The cliffs made a fairly steep decline all the way to the water's edge. It was so peaceful, so organic – the views and tranquility were second to none. Annoyed, I pulled around and went back to the street and was able to park half on the street and half up on the curb.

I thought, "Okay God, you wanted me to come here, so here I am." I waited for God to show up and of course He didn't. Impatiently, I decided to leave. And when I started to back up, I heard God say "I told you to go here."

I started talking out loud and said, "God, there are no

parking spaces here!" The words had barely left my mouth when right in front of me a car backed up, leaving a parking space available right in front of me. I pulled in the space and got out of the truck.

Flying overhead, seabirds drifted and crisscrossed over the rocky outcroppings below me. Some people had made their way around the fence line and were sitting on the sandstone. No way was I going down there. I sat there and prayed as I waited and listened for what God had in mind. I was still waiting for someone to tell me I was supposed to be a pastor. After what seemed like an eternity (probably all of five minutes), again I determined it was time to be going. Again, God stopped me. He reminded me that I needed to have eyes to see. So I started looking around.

As my eyes wandered, I noticed a woman sitting about 100 yards down the slope on a little outcropping of sandstone. I couldn't see what she was doing because she had her back to me, but she appeared to be very tranquil and looking out over the ocean.

I clearly heard, "Go down there and talk to her." I thought to myself, "I don't need to go down there." I replied, "God, if you want her to talk to me send her up here to me." I heard Him say, "Don't test me, I told you to go down there and talk to her." Sighing, I climbed over the fence and headed down the rocks.

Okay, picture this: Here is a woman alone, sitting with her back to me because she's looking at the view. She is a solitary figure, I assume by choice. Now, there's a man (me) walking up behind her and about to interrupt her peace. What do you say in a situation like this? How do you break the ice? Thoughts were racing through my mind. Time to tighten that belt to trust God and what HE knows.

Remember, I have been fasting for three days. My filter is off and I am wide open with saying what ever I hear. My opening words to the woman stun even me as they cross my lips. "Hello. The Lord Jesus Christ sent me down here to talk to you." There. It. Is. What can her response possibly be? Would she chuck a shoe at me? Tell me to get lost? Scream?

Unexpectedly, she looked at me kind of awed, yet perplexed and said "Really? Please sit down." As I sat down, I noticed an open Bible in her lap. As if that were the trigger, she began to speak right away. As with all the others that weekend, she easily talked about what was on her mind. For 20 minutes, she talked about how she had been sitting there reading the Bible and admitted she really didn't understand what she was reading. She was confused about what it took to be a Christian. She had asked God to send somebody to help her understand. Just as she finished her prayer, she looked up and there I was. In her mind, I was the one He had sent. I think she mistakenly assumed I might be an angel. Fat chance of that. I was far from angelic.

With gentle assurance, I ministered to her and I explained the free gift of salvation from the Word of God. I saw when she made the connection in her own Bible; when she realized there was nothing she could do to earn salvation because it was a free gift. Tears flowed and she expressed her joy. It was time to go, so I suggested we pray. Afterwards, we said our goodbyes and she thanked me for taking the time to speak with her. (Thank God for that one!) I worked my way back up the hillside, struggling a little because my legs were tired. My whole attitude was tired. Back in my truck, I started it up and began a conversation with God. Frankly, I was annoyed.

"God, I don't get it.   All weekend, I had something for everyone. Yet no one had anything for me. When I came here there was supposed to be some sort of sign that I was supposed to let all my construction business go so I could focus on pastoring."   Once I stopped talking, it became very quiet in the cab of my truck. I was alone with my thoughts which were running every which way. Then He spoke, "Son, don't you get it?" He said, "That is the sign." "All you've done the whole time you've been here is pastoring."

He couldn't have been clearer. The past three days had been a glimpse of my future. Being obedient when the Father spoke to me was what he was trying to show me.

That evening from the plane I watched the sun set behind the Pacific horizon, which painted the perfect dramatic end for my trip. I left San Diego with no concrete understanding of where my path would take me. Amazingly, it didn't bother me because I finally realized that my future was not mine, it was His. I needed to forget the reality of my past and grasp on to the truth of what His plans were for me. I decided to go back to submit myself to my pastor and align myself with whatever work he wanted me to do. I trusted God would speak through him also.

So, are there things that I wish I knew before I became a pastor? Nope. Not knowing kept me seeking after God. Heck, I didn't even know that I didn't know. Luckily, God did. His words of truth eventually became my reality and I became a pastor.

Buckle Up, Not Buckle Under

Now, as a wise old coot, I don't choose to hear any words spoken over me that do not echo my Maverick Mentor's voice. I choose instead to speak His words of truth over myself. "I am the healed. I am the delivered. I am the forgiven."

I have clearly heard my God tell me that He has already healed me and that it just has not manifested physically yet. But in time it will and it will be for His Glory. Until then, I wait upon Him and His timing. (Ephesians 3:20 – Now to him who is able to do immeasurably more than all we ask or imagine, according to His power that is at work within us.)

The epic battle for reality starts in the mind. Truth is the antidote to the poison of this world's thinking. Even though my legs were giving out in the natural. I was standing like a giant in the supernatural because on some days, the only standing I could do was to **"Stand Firm Upon the Truth of the Word of God so You Can Buckle Up - Not Buckle Under - Reality."** That is **lesson three** from my Maverick Mentor.

Round Up Questions:

1.) What is the difference between Reality and Truth?

2.) Describe a time when you secretly did a good thing for someone and did not let them know who did it.

3.) When have you felt like you were buckling under? Did you feel like God was giving you more than you could handle? What did you do?

4.) How have you buckled up and stood on the truth of the Word of God?

5.) What secret has God whispered over your life that you need to stand upon?

CHAPTER 5

"Walk in the Boots that were Fashioned for You"

Struggles that Strengthen

Actors have worn them and so have Presidents - and for that matter, so have actors who became Presidents. Most men, though, will go through life without ever having tried a cowboy boot on. My advice? Don't be that guy.

Boots were an integral part of westerns. One of my most intense memories of seeing cowboy boots in a movie was in *Hang 'Em High*. In the opening scene, the cowboy, Jed Cooper, drove a herd of cattle across a river. As he was about to exit the water on his horse, he heard the lowing of a baby calf in distress who has gotten stuck in the riverbed. He turned back and jumped into the water, cowboy boots and all. "I am gonna have to carry you, huh?" he said to the baby calf. Tromping through the water in his cowboy boots, he brought the calf safely to the other side.

(My mom would have killed me for ruining good footwear but Clint Eastwood didn't give it a second thought.)

In the distance, a band of riders converged on the opposite side of the riverbank and plunged across towards Jed and his herd. They accused Jed of rustling the cattle. He couldn't convince the nine men of his innocence so they acted as judge and jury right on the spot. Forming a lynch mob, they set up a noose in a tree and the ringleader gave the command: "Hang 'em. Hang 'em high."

As a young kid I sat stunned as the opening movie credits flashed across Clint Eastwood's wet dripping boots as he dangles from a tree branch with a noose cutting into the flesh around his neck. I recognized those were the same boots that Clint wore as his character, Rowdy, in the television series, Rawhide.

"What? We are only seven minutes into the movie and my hero is dead and left dangling in a tree?" My heart pounded as I watch those boots spin round and round. Just minutes before, he was charging out in those bold boots to rescue an immature calf from certain death and now those same boots hung limply from his lifeless legs.

What irony! Just as he helped the calf get through its struggle, he entered an even greater struggle himself. (Spoiler alert: He doesn't die. He returns as a lawman to hunt down his lynch mob and bring them to justice). I started to wonder, "What is it about struggles that strengthens my resolve?"

Let's Get Bold

I'm typing and talking to God at the same time. I asked God for a download on who in the Bible went through struggles. I grabbed the Bible and opened it to the Table of Contents. God said "Just start reading the names," I read out loud, "Adam, Cain, Moses, Joseph, Jacob, Ruth, Samuel, Ezra, Nehemiah, Ester, Job, Solomon, Isaiah, Jeremiah, Elijah, Elisha, Ezekiel, Daniel, Meshach, Shadrack and Abendigo. Hosea, Joel, Amos, Obadiah, Jonah, Micah, Nahum, Habbakkuk, Zephaniah, Haggai, Zechariah, Malachi, John the Baptist, JESUS, The apostle Paul - ALL of them."

He said, "Do you see? To make it into my book you have to do it my way. Even with the struggles...Be BOLD!" Now I got it. If you wanted to be like these guys, you had to be bold. They all fought. They all were in the arena. None of them watched from the stands. All of them walked out the hard lessons that fashioned them into the men and women God designed them to be. They were able to excel in the battle because they were not barefoot, but ready to stand their ground. When you are told to stand, you make sure you have the footwear to keep you upright.

The Gospel (The Good News) of Peace is symbolized by sturdy, protective shoes. (More like steel-toed boots, not flip flops). Just as there are all types of boots, there are all types of wearers. Boots make you walk a certain way. Maybe they even make you swagger. I must confess, it makes me draw up the mental image of Nancy Sinatra singing, "These boots are made for walking, and that's just what they'll do. One of these days these boots are gonna..." (Google it).

There is a certain amount of boldness in a boot, especially a boot that is fashioned just for the wearer. But my boots were meant to usher in the Gospel of Peace. Satan scatters traps for us as we're trying to spread the gospel. The Gospel of Peace is our protection, reminding us that it is by grace that souls are saved. We can sidestep Satan's obstacles when we remember "For God so loved the world that He gave His one and only Son, that whoever believes in Him shall not perish but have eternal life." (John 3:16, NIV) The Gospel of Peace started for me when I found a peace with God and accepted the work His Son did for me on the cross. When I asked him to forgive me of all my selfish ways, He brought a new peace to my life. I was in right standing with my Creator. I could not help but share the good news of that newfound peace with people in my life. The Gospel of Peace is described in 1 Peter 3:15 like this: "... always be ready to give a defense to everyone who asks you a reason for the hope that is in you, with meekness and fear ..." (NIV) Sharing the gospel of salvation ultimately brings peace between God and men (Romans 5:1). My boldness didn't come right away, though. There was one day when I had a dream from God and I wasn't bold enough to share it.

I Had A Dream

I had a dream. But this was an ugly dream. A man died. I didn't know anything about the man except that he was the father of one of the students in my S.C.U.B.A. Basic Open Water Certification class.

When I woke up, I knew that I was supposed to tell this girl in my class that her father was going to die. I could not get back to sleep. Surely, his death was not really going to happen. But somehow I knew it was very real. And God was asking me to share that information with this girl before her certification party on the weekend.

"Ummm, no way." I had barely had any contact with this girl during the six weeks of the class and their Mexico trip. Now I was supposed to walk up and tell her that her father was going to die? How could God ask me to do something like that?

Since I've been a believer, I've seen many ways in which the Lord has touched my life. For me it's been 25+ years of trying to live God's way. So much of my life has been a learning process of how to be obedient to do what I hear God telling me to do. Accepting His way has made the miraculous very normal in my life. But it didn't start off so easy, I was a new-to-the-faith baby believer. This one was a FAIL. Sort of.

As the class Dive Master, I had taken the group from Tempe, Arizona to the Mexico coast to certify them in open water diving. The trip had marked the completion of the class, so when we returned home to Arizona, they all knew there would be an official celebration party where the certification cards would be given to them.

Two days before the party, I had the dream that Amy's father would pass away. I agonized over what to do. I tried to understand WHY God would want me to tell her this. Would she even want to know in advance?

To be honest, I just couldn't imagine telling someone this kind of terrible news, even if I was absolutely sure it was true. Reasoning with myself, I formed a plan. I knew that I would see Amy at the certification party on the following day, so I decided I would just wait and possibly tell her then. Really, I was giving myself some more time. Certainly, it wasn't what God said to do, but I was young and inexperienced in the ways of God.

Party day came and I went to the dive shop. When I arrived I said hello to all of our students and noticed Amy was not there. I inquired about her only to learn that she had a "family emergency" in California and would not be at the dive shop to receive her open water diver certification.

I FREAKED. I knew what the family emergency was. I had the dream about it 2 nights before. My heart sank. I prayed like mad that it wasn't her dad, but I already knew it was.

Amy was gone for a week. Word spread at the dive shop that her father had passed away and she was home for the funeral. I don't mind admitting, the guilt factor was high because I had not given her the heads up like God had instructed me. "Oh man, what if it had been her last chance to talk to him and then didn't get to because I was disobedient?   Why did I chicken out?"

In the week that she was gone, I felt like I was waiting at the door (not really, but it felt that way). When she did come back to Arizona, I called and invited her to lunch. At this point, it had been about ten days since his passing and I needed to clear my conscience. The weight of this pre-knowledge was so heavy and I wanted to repent to her in person for not giving her the heads up to say goodbye to her father. Little did I know, God had part two of the plan for Amy. I was going to be instrumental in it.

We met at a restaurant and barely had a minute to sit down before I launched right in to the conversation. (I was not a guy to beat around the bush). I stared directly at her and said "Please forgive me for what I'm about to say." (Nice start, Mr. Sensitive!)

She looked at me and waited patiently, while in my head I was thinking, "I've only really known her for a few weeks. In fact, she was only an acquaintance, a student of mine."

I began again, "I don't mean to hurt you in any way, but on the Wednesday before our certification party, I had a dream that your father passed away and I was supposed to tell you about it on Thursday before it happened, but I was too scared to say anything." She just blinked.

Quickly, I went on about how much God loved her and how He tried to use me to tell her about this upcoming tragedy. I apologized again that I had not given her the information so she could say goodbye. "I'm so sorry that I didn't tell you," I said.

She looked at me with wide eyes and tears just exploded. She started to speak, but couldn't. I sat there looking down at my hands in my lap, not really knowing what to say at this point. I began to babble on.

I told her of God's goodness and His mercy but all the while I felt like a failure. Ever known you are doing a miserable job in proclaiming the Lord because your own life is a sorry example? That is how I felt.

Why hadn't I listened? How could she believe in Him when I couldn't even do what He asked? My words sounded hollow even to me as I choked them out.

Swallowing, I composed myself and sent up a little flare prayer asking God to speak clearly through me. Again, I told her of the love of her heavenly Father and how much He wanted a relationship with her. After a few minutes of talking, I looked up and she was nodding in agreement. Encouraged, I kept going. Supernaturally, God must have said the words through me that she needed to hear.

Through a cascade of tears, she asked me to please help her accept Jesus into her heart. "What? How could that be? Even when I didn't do such a great job representing Him, His love for her shone through."

Well, I wasn't going to mess this part up, so right there on the spot in the middle of a busy restaurant I had her recite the sinners prayer while I held her hands. Amy was welcomed into the family of God. It was so awesome!

Afterwards, Amy quietly said, "You know, you are

actually the second person to tell me about my dad." She went on to tell me that the first person did tell her on Thursday. Although it freaked her out, she had been able to call her dad and have a lengthy conversation with him. Stunned, I was so relieved! I thought I had screwed everything up when I didn't tell her as God instructed, but He put Plan B into action.

Wouldn't you know it? God knew I wouldn't pull it off and He had backed me up! How amazing is that? Plan B involved allowing me a second chance to be a part of Amy's story. Because I felt so guilty about not telling her about the dream, I had felt compelled to meet with Amy to ask her forgiveness after her father's death. God turned that repentance conversation into a wonderful miracle of salvation conversation. God is always redeeming our failures into successes while teaching us about His heart.

To this day, I believe very much if you don't do what God asks you to do, He will probably find somebody else to complete His plan. But He will always find a way to take repentance to another level of understanding. I was very hard on myself and felt like I was sinning against the Lord. In this case, God brought me into an event knowing that I would fail at telling Amy about the dream. But even so, He bestowed a greater gift upon me by allowing me to be a part of Amy's salvation prayer. It was a very real dream come true holding her hand as she walked through the door of salvation. Thank you Lord for taking my mess and making it into your message.

"The LORD makes firm the steps of the one who delights in Him; though he may stumble, he will not fall, for the LORD upholds him with His hand." Psalm 37:23-24

I was too hesitant to put on my cowboy boots of boldness that morning but luckily I had them with me. My

Maverick Mentor must have been chuckling watching me drag those things around with me. "Why don't you just WEAR them?" Honestly, I hadn't broken them in yet and they felt awkward. Sharing my story of how I came to know Jesus felt awkward, telling others of God's plan of salvation felt awkward and sometimes just praying for people felt awkward. There are days when I asked myself, "If I had been tole as a young man this is how my life with Christ was going to be, would I have chosen it?" In my ignorance, I probably would have gone a different direction. But now that I've gone this direction for all these years, I would never go back again. Why? I've become a personal friend with my mentor, Jesus, and all the awkwardness is gone. Since I have walked so many miles in them, my boots of the gospel fit me like a glove.

This life has brought me into such an intimate relationship with my Creator and sustained and comforted and GROWN me into a man that I am so grateful to be. I know that Christ has not caused my disabilities, but I have allowed Him to use my struggles to refine and tool me into a godly man. For that, I am grateful too. I always had the choice not to choose Him. I wanted to be a maverick, a real cowboy, and they wore boots. Not just any boots, but BOLD boots. Now, let me tell you about some boots.

What Men Wear

I used to have boots of every kind. Cowboy boots made of every kind of skin: boa, ostrich, and alligator. Tall boots with supple leather uppers and square-toed boots with rings and spurs. Hard-edged work boots and boots for motorcycle riding. Boots were to me, what heels were to my wife. There was a different pair for every occasion. More than that, each pair made me walk a bit differently.

One day when I was young in my faith, came a moment in my walk with God that I would not soon forget. I was working construction in Hawaii. Cowboy boots had given way to cooler shoes like loafers and topsiders. I moved in my characteristic fast-pace as the Vice President of a local construction company. During my noon hour, I stopped at a local plate-lunch place to grab a bite to eat. As usual, I had a hundred different things on my mind as I parked my Jag and began my walk to the entrance. Holding the door for a little old man who was shuffling out with a walker, I barely registered him on my consciousness.

There was no line so I quickly got my food and found a table by the front window where I could watch my car. I was absorbed in my own thoughts, but I noticed the same little man with the walker struggle slowly past the cars in the parking lot. My heart went out to him. There, in the "holy moment" of unwrapping my food, God spoke to me. "If you go pray for him, I'll heal him." I'm sitting there holding my sandwich thinking, "What? Right NOW?" I had just sat down with my food, the time clock was ticking, and I was hungry. So I began this ridiculous argument with God. "What if I go out there and get his hopes up? What if I pray and nothing happens? What if he thinks I'm a nut? What if he won't let me pray for him?" I even had the selfish thought, "What if you heal him and my day gets even MORE off track?"

Well, as always, God won the argument. I would like to say that I moved with cheerful obedience, but I didn't. With somewhat of an attitude, I got up from the table, left my food behind and headed for the door. Once outside I looked in the direction the man had been not more than a few minutes before, but now he was nowhere in sight. I hustled around the rows of cars sure that I would see him there. Nope. Bewildered now, I looked up and down the street, but he was gone. He had disappeared. Are you kidding? How far could he go? No way had he outpaced me. My head was spinning – had he even been real or was he just a test of my obedience?

I slowly returned to the restaurant. My attitude had changed a lot by the time I got back to my table. Part of me felt relieved that I would not have to awkwardly pray over him there in the parking lot. All those "What if…'s" were turning into "What would have…'s". I pushed my uneaten food aside as feelings of remorse took hold. God told me to do something and I didn't walk in faith. It was like I was wearing cement shoes when He asked me.

What really got me was that I COULD HAVE done something that could have opened the door to healing for that man. Instead I was selfish. I was frightened that I might look foolish. Worried that God might not talk to me again, I prayed for the man anyway, but did it silently in my head. I even prayed that God would give the man a second chance for healing by asking someone else who was more obedient than me to pray for him. It didn't seem enough.

I decided then and there if God would give me another opportunity, I would never shy away again. Those cement shoes had to go. I was a boot man. I had this mental image of me putting on some BOLD BOOTS. Kind of like cowboy boots but they were specifically to take dominion where God would call me to go. They gave me a fearless confidence that whatever God asked, He would put the power to it. It wasn't my job to DO the impossible, it was just my job to BELIEVE. So I prayed, "Lord, please don't take this gift away – give me another chance to do Your will. My bold boots are on."

Since then, God has given me several opportunities to wear the bold boots of faith. When I first began, I used to pull them on and off as needed. Eventually, I decided it was just easier to wear them all the time. Now, even though my walking in boots has temporarily halted in the natural because of the loss of the use of my legs, I am able to walk in those boots in the supernatural every day.

Today, when I look down to bow my head to pray, there they are. No one sees them but me and God, but it gives me comfort to know that He trusts me with opportunities to walk in those bold boots of faith.

Let's face it. Sometimes we all want to cowboy it up a little. Western boots come from a long tradition of American independence and manhood. Like Clint Eastwood, I have a little swagger when I have my boots on. Thankfully, I don't have to put on the bold boots anymore. It is because I never take them off. My boots are on all the time. They have been worn in and fashioned just for me. They are as comfortable as house slippers. When I get the opportunity to spread the gospel of peace, the boots take me there. Like the time I met this little leprechaun of a man in a lime-green leisure suit. My mentor had taught me well and I was about to be his game-changer.

Lime Green Suit

It was a magical balmy day in Honolulu at my coffee shop. It was one of those signature days in Hawaii with lots of sunshine and bright blue skies that stretched out endless miles over the ocean. I was sitting outside on the patio lanai. Over the rim of my coffee cup, I could see people going about their day in this tropical paradise. I liked to read my Bible here because it was very peaceful, a very tranquil place, and very spiritual. I lifted my head just as the cool ocean breeze embraced my face and looked up to see the white puffy clouds blow by – I was humbled and quietly thanked my Father for his creation.

I was distracted by the sound of sobbing. I looked over and saw an old man probably in his 80's, dressed in a bright lime-green leisure suit. He had shuffled up to an outdoor table on my cafe patio with a woman. She got him situated and with a pat on the back, left him and headed to the restroom.

Intrigued by his colorful outfit, I observed him more closely. Simply put, he was a sobbing mess. Clearly he was very upset. I love the Lord, so I sent up a flare prayer for the guy. God said (and I heard him clearly), "If you go over there and pray for him, I will heal him." My heart started pounding hard as I instantly remembered that time years before when God spoke to me this way. The remorse for not putting on my bold boots and doing as I was asked came flooding back. I looked at the man again – I had no idea what was up, but it was time to be obedient and move in faith.

I walked over to the guy and said, "My name is Rob Moore and the Lord Jesus Christ sent me over here to tell you that I need to pray for you and He'd heal you, so what's up?" The man needed no prodding. Through tears he explained he had cancer. He had just come from his oncologist who told him they had taken the treatment as far as they could, there wasn't anything more they could do – he had 30 days to live.

I thought to myself, "Oh boy, here we go!" I said to him, "I serve the God that created everything and if He wants to heal you, He'll heal you right now. Can I pray for you?" Still caught up in his despair, he just shrugged and said, "Sure, go ahead." I got the feeling he was not feeling me or this situation. Nevertheless, I moved forward. I kept a small vial of anointing oil on my key chain so I put a little drop on his forehead, put my hand on his head, closed my eyes and started praying.

I want you to know it was INCREDIBLE! I could feel heat in my hands and the Holy Spirit in my heart. After praying, I opened my eyes and the guy looked 20 years younger. I'm telling you, sitting right in front of me, right before my eyes. . . the man looked 20 YEARS YOUNGER! He had stopped crying and was looking straight at me.

I watched his eyes grow wide as the knowing came over him. He first shook his head and then shook his whole body, as if to shake off invisible, binding, heavy chains.

The effect had clearly overwhelmed him and he shouted, "I FEEL GREAT! I FEEL FABULOUS. I CAN'T BELIEVE IT. I'M HEALED!!!"

His excitement got the attention of his care-giver who had just returned from the inside of the cafe. She walked over to the table and said, "What in the world is going on here?" She was talking to me, but staring at him. Her eyes were wide with disbelief. He did not look like the man I had walked up to a few minutes before. His countenance had changed. The old, beaten, broken, distraught man of a few minutes ago had been replaced by his younger Spirit man who was shining brightly through.

Despite his age, the man quickly stood up, pointed at me, and said to her, "This man came over to me and said, 'My God wants to heal you if you are willing." With confidence he continued, "I said, 'Go ahead.' and he prayed for me. With a loud clap of his hands he said, "God HEALED me. I NO LONGER HAVE CANCER!!" She stood there shaking her head, clearly perplexed.

The man turned back to me and asked "Please tell me more about this Jesus Christ." We spent some time together and he listened intently as I shared Jesus with him. It seemed like the world passed by that table without either of us looking up to take notice. I knew I had his attention. Before long, the man in the lime-green leisure suit decided to accept Jesus Christ as His Lord and Savior – it was a game changer. Praise the Lord!

I have to tell you in my life, I had never seen anything like that. You have to understand that this was a man probably in his 80's who now looked like he was in his 60's. My mind was filled with the wonder of it all as I watched them walk away. As if God himself was saluting me, the old man jumped up and clicked his heels together. That was the last thing I saw as they got in their car and drove away. I was so blown away, but could not help myself and enjoyed a hearty, grateful laugh! God you are so cool!

I realize the power is NOT me or even IN me. The power is ALL HIM. The power is based on moving forward on what He said to do and when He said to do it. I no longer had to look around for my bold boots to put on because now I was wearing them all the time. The more you wear them, the more you break them in. The more broken in they are, the more they fit your feet perfectly. The more perfectly they fit you, the more comfortable they are. It also makes it very hard for anyone else to walk in your boots because they become so fashioned for you and you alone. So often, we want to walk in someone else's' boots and then wonder why they are so uncomfortable for us. I have learned to always be ready to go. I want to be the guy that's available and doing it His way – ALL the time. He was able to use me because I was wearing the boots of the Gospel of Peace that were fashioned just for me.

How do I know that? That first time when God asked me to share a dream, I had no faith and chickened out of telling my friend about her dad. The next time, at lunch, when God asked me to put on my bold boots and pray for the man with the walker, my faith was still immature. Plus, God's request didn't really fit my agenda for the day. I was still learning my agenda should always be His agenda. After I've matured a bit, the next time God gave me the opportunity I DID NOT HESITATE and I became a game changer for the man after his doctor's appointment. I already had my bold boots on because I don't take them off much anymore. I didn't know the old man in the lime-green leisure suit, but both of our lives are changed forever because of my boots.

Each of us have our own walk with God. Each of us has a process to go through to mature spiritually. I call this struggle, "Staying in my own lane." You may not be an actor or a President, but God has some spiritual boots for you to walk in that were fitted just for you. Time to slip them on and break them in.

"Walk in the boots that were fashioned for you" is **lesson four** from my *Maverick Mentor*.

Round Up Questions:

1.) When have you thought it was all over....and then realized it was just the beginning?

2.) What struggles have strengthened you?

3.) How has the gospel brought peace between you and God?

4.) Describe a time when you have been bold enough to share your faith.

5.) How is God showing you to stay in your own lane and walk in the boots that were fashioned for you?

CHAPTER 6

"How to See Farther"

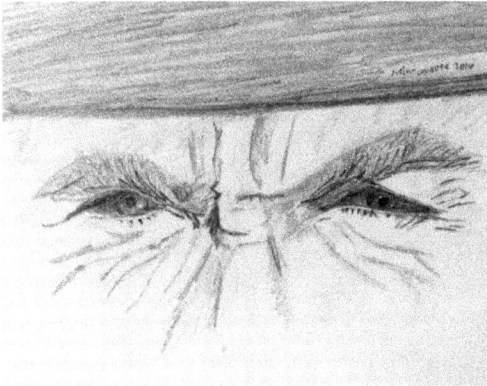

See Farther

"A good glare can be just as effective as a gun..." Clint
Eastwood

Every once in a while, actors think they have to scrunch
up their eyes while being on screen. It seems to be a way of
increasing the badass level of the character they are playing. It
certainly worked for Clint Eastwood. His glare alone could
extinguish the enemy's attack. It also allowed him to see farther
and anticipate what was coming.

In the movie *High Plains Drifter*, a distant figure on
horseback rides through simmering, midday heat. As he comes
nearer, we see a bearded man in a dark cowboy hat and long
dusty overcoat. The Stranger enters the tiny western town of
Lago and rides slowly down the main street. The townspeople

stop and watch him pass. One significant foreshadow is the look he gives the undertaker as he surveys his available coffins.

The Stranger has squinted into the future to see what is about to come. They didn't know his face and they didn't know his name, but they would never forget the day he drifted into town. True to the foreshadowing, the Drifter places more than a few men in the undertaker's grasp that day. He never doubted, because he could squint to see the future. It was his shield of faith.

Our shield of faith guards us against one of Satan's deadliest weapons, doubt. Satan shoots doubt at us when God does not act immediately or visibly. But our faith in God's trustworthiness comes from the unassailable truth of the Bible. We know we can count on our Father. Our Shield of Faith sends Satan's flaming arrows of doubt glancing harmlessly to the side. We keep our shield held high, confident in the knowledge that God provides, God protects, and God is faithful to His children. Our shield holds because of our faith in the One, Jesus Christ.

Squinting helps us to see better by changing the shape of our eye which changes our perception. Faith for a believer is like a squint towards the future. You squint to change perception of your faith to believe differently.

Here is a Biblical definition of faith: "the substance of things hoped for, the evidence of things not seen." (Hebrews 11:1, NIV)

It is tangible, not some hazy emotion without being grounded in reality. Faith is real. Though it is based on solid evidence, that doesn't mean it comes naturally to me or even easily. Honestly, faith involves a huge amount of trust. You don't hope for what you already have.

A maverick already takes an independent stand apart from his associates and doesn't see the same way that others see. My Maverick Mentor had to show me that even mavericks have to unlearn some things the world has taught you in order to have true child-like faith.

Wheel of Favor

AN IDIOM: ***"par for the course"***
Definition #1:   ***typical; about what one could expect.***

I am a learned man. I graduated summa cum laude from the school of hard knocks. I am streetwise and experienced in the ways of the world. But God taught me that there were two things I needed to UNLEARN to understand favor in His kingdom. (Favor could be defined as a Divine Assigned Advantage For Success.) It goes against all the playbooks I had learned growing up. My thinking was typical; par for the course; about what one could expect.

Let me tell you how my son taught me my 'Maverick Mentor's lesson' on F A I T H.

One of my many favorite pastimes is playing the game "Wheel of Fortune" particularly when my son Jordan was very young. I'd gather him up and we'd watch the game show on television when I got home from work. It was our time to spend together. Amazingly, my six-year old solved many of the puzzles before I could figure them out. Since it was a wildly popular show, it was only a matter of time before "Wheel of Fortune" came to Hawaii for a taping. It was announced during the show that they were looking for contestants on Oahu. Jordan immediately declared that I should be on the show. Really? Maybe him, my little brainiac son, but not me.

I was just a street smart construction worker who loved

to hang out with his kid. I chuckled at the thought of me even trying out for the show. But Jordan was so insistent that I said, "Okay, I will check it out."

To try out for the show, you had to fill out an application. Every day when I got home, Jordan would remind me about it. On the last day applications were being accepted, we were driving to church. Jordan asked, "Dad, did you ever fill out an application? Today is the last day." This kid never forgot anything. He sounded so hopeful that I almost couldn't admit that I hadn't done it. I assured him I was going to go fill one out that very day.

On our way home, I stopped at the huge outdoor Royal Hawaiian Shopping Center in Waikiki to get an application. As you might have guessed; when you wait until the last day to accomplish something, you better be prepared to pay the price. The first little shop I stopped at had given away all their applications but suggested another shop that might have some left. For the next 45 minutes, while my family sat in the car waiting, I was bounced from shop to shop in pursuit of an application.

I finally ended up at a tobacco smoke shop. They actually had one left. It was probably the last application on the planet. Eureka! I quickly filled it out and handed it to the clerk behind the store counter. Just as quickly, he gave it back to me. He told me I had to officially submit it at the office kiosk in the mall courtyard which was at the opposite end of the mall from where I started. Great! I had more walking to do.

I made my way to the administrative area only to find the office was closed on Sundays. With a quick prayer to God, I folded the paper and slid it under the door. There. It was done! Relieved, I returned to the car and told my son I had filled out the application and turned it in. He bounced up and down with excitement. "Daddy's gonna win! Daddy's gonna win!"

Yeah, right. Just getting called in for an audition would be a long shot. Winning would be a miracle! Honestly, I didn't even think anyone in the kiosk would notice the paper on the floor.

The next night on the TV news, we learned that over 18,000 people had applied to get on the show. My son's big blue eyes radiated confidence when he said "I'm going to pray for you every day, Daddy!" Sure enough, that night before bed I heard my son's earnest prayer asking God to let his daddy be the big winner at Wheel of Fortune. I smiled at his childish faith. I had none. He was faith-FULL; I was skeptical.

About a week went by. I received a phone call that out of the 18,000 entries, I happened to be one of the 1000 being called in for an audition. "Are you kidding me?"

My son was so excited! He followed me around that day, giving me test puzzles to solve. It was his way of helping me prepare. I didn't have the heart to tell him that it was just a random drawing from the properly filled out entries. Truly it was the "luck of the draw."

The day of the audition I showed up bright and early along with several hundred other hopefuls. It was a full day of activity with each of us getting a chance to stand before a panel to spin the wheel. What was the panel looking for? I didn't have a clue. They had some special formula of what made a good contestant and they were keeping mum about what that secret mix was. At the end of the day, all we were given was, "We'll let you know."

From this point, the notifications came daily. First, I was

notified that I made the cut to 400. I needed to drop everything and be at the next interview the following morning. Those 400 people sat in a room and tried to solve puzzles on the big board. For some reason, the puzzles seemed easy to me and I was always one of the first to raise my hand with an answer when they turned over a letter.

As the day came to a close and I prepared to be dismissed, I learned I made the cut to be one of 120 who were moving on to the next round. At the 120 interview, the tone completely changed. The Wheel Of Fortune contestant search team explained that from here the cuts would be quick and decisive. Each of the 120 people was asked to show their enthusiasm and personality to the team.

Within the hour, we were slashed to the Top 30 but we were not told who made the cut. To be top 30 meant you were either one of 15 actual players or one of 15 alternates. We were told that if you had made Top 30, you would be notified the next morning, which was Sunday.

Honestly, I was pretty thrilled with the prospect. I had not really thought through making it this far. Although this was such a unique experience and I was having fun, I hadn't anticipated taking this much time off of work. But when they said wait by the phone on Sunday – I snapped to attention. I raised my hand and said, "I won't be around on Sunday morning because I'll be at church." They advised me that if I really wanted a spot, I better stay home and stick by the phone. I simply said to myself, "Well, that's not going to happen. God is going to be a priority over a game." Jordan would just have to understand. (Note to reader: this was a time before the whole world had a cell phone).

God blessed my loyalty. He didn't make me wait until

Sunday morning. Saturday night around 7 p.m., I received a phone call from the Wheel Of Fortune producer. "Mr. Moore, Congratulations!! You have been selected as one of the top 30 players – can you be available to play?"

What? He was saying I had been selected for Top 30? Are you kidding me? This was a dream. He asked again, "Can you play?"

I said, "Sure," but I could only think about Jordan's face when I told him the news. After a brief pause, he said, "You won't find out if you are one of the players or the alternate until right before you are asked to go on air." My heart was soaring, I already knew I was a player. There was no doubt now. My son's magnificent outrageous prayer was being answered. His dad was going to be on Wheel of Fortune.

Playing on Wheel of Fortune in Hawaii

One of my greatest joys as a father was when I was able to tell my son the big news. My thoughtful bride recorded it on our handheld VHS for all eternity. Jordan jumped and screamed, "I knew it! I knew it! My dad is going to win Wheel of Fortune!" His belief didn't seem so outrageous to me now. I really did feel a confidence, a "God-fidence" that something amazing was going to happen.

The following Monday my son Jordan sat in the audience with my wife as I was selected to play for a nationally televised audience on Wheel of Fortune, the most popular game show in the world. Yes, Jordan was right. I was the BIG winner.

Although I didn't guess the final puzzle, I shook hands with Pat Sajak and kissed Vanna White on the cheek Hawaiian-style. (My dad got a big kick out of that.) The moment seemed surreal but it elevated my expectations of just what God could do for a kid with faith.

AN IDIOM: **"par for the course"**

Definition #2: **what should be expected because of past experience**

Overall, the experience was fun and exciting but the lasting, defining moment in all of it was the faith of my son. Before Wheel of Fortune, I was sure that there was no way that I would be selected out of 18,000 entries to be one of the players. I also had been taught that you do what you know and stick with your abilities.

My son's prayer and my experience on Wheel of Fortune turned all that earthly education on its ear. One of the puzzles that I solved was "PAR FOR THE COURSE" which is an idiom meaning "Typical, or what is expected." That doesn't describe a maverick at all.

The alternate definition for PAR FOR THE COURSE" is "What should be expected because of past experience."

That second definition is now how I see my future. After my debut and win on Wheel of Fortune, I consider miracles to be "par for the course." I expect to see God do the miraculous in spite of my abilities. It all started with those two things I had to unlearn to understand faith. First, have the faith of a child, not a jaded adult. Second, it is not my will, but the Father's will to be done while I am here on earth. Miracles are now "par for the course."

Squinting towards the future God shows me, I have to believe what I have not yet seen. It is my shield of faith from the attack of the enemy. My squint wards off the oncoming foe. Have you ever given your kids "the look?" It says, "Go ahead, make my day." My squint can even back off an adult male from the direction he's headed. When I add my "truth" telling from God, it can definitely become a shield of faith.

Squint for Others

I am not always good at filtering what my mouth speaks when I am in "God-Mode" so I am sure that sometimes I sound pretty ridiculous. I am just speaking from the perspective of knowing WHO holds someone's future.

One afternoon, I was having a mentorship lunch with a young man I was discipling. He was an employee at a local bank branch and doing pretty well. Our conversation turned to the future and God's dreams for him. All of a sudden, I was speaking something totally out of left field over him.

Even to my ears, it was something so totally radically different than the life that he was living. It was the voice of the maverick in me. I knew it might have sounded kind of radical to someone who didn't believe the power of God causes dreams to come true. He had never been on Wheel of Fortune. His faith was low. I could tell by the puzzled look on his face that he was wondering where in the world I was coming up with this. Honestly, I felt like God was speaking through me. I continued speaking his future, just like my little Jordan spoke over mine.

Fast forward one year and this young man sent me the following message:

Hey! First of all ... Happy Fathers Day Rob!

I wanted to let you know that as of Wednesday, I am an official certified personal trainer through the NFPT organization. I studied hard for it and I am excited! I tell you this because I don't think I would have pursued this line of business had it not been for God working through you. After you prophesied to me at lunch on 3.11.11, the following day I received a magazine in the mail addressed to the wrong person. It was a personal trainer magazine. My roommate and I had lived at the apartment for about eight months and we had never received ANY magazines like that.

Additionally, I had several co-workers from the bank mention to me that very week that I should be a personal trainer which seemed to be out of nowhere. With that confirmation, I knew you were right and I was supposed to pursue personal training as my passion and dream.

So ... right now I'm still at the bank but have the necessary education credentials (and physique!) to pursue personal training. I just put a request into corporate to allow me to work full time at the bank and part-time at a local health club. I want to build up some experience and also help people on the side. I have several people at church who want me to train them.

Our talks inspired me on naming my dream vocation something that reflects my journey. I plan on calling my business "Metanoia Fitness" ... Metanoia is a greek word that means to have a change of heart, to change your beliefs about something, or to change the way you think. It comes from the word "repent." Thank BOTH you and your wife for pouring into my life for several seasons. I love you both so much.

Today this young man is a personal trainer who caters towards people with disabilities and special needs just as God showed me. He is pursuing his unique, God-given talents and ambitions. His shield is up and he is squinting towards his future.

It wasn't me that spurred him on. All I said was something downloaded by God. But that's what I do. I disregard what the world sees and narrow my eyes into a good glare. It is pretty easy when I am seeing the future by squinting for someone else. It is much more difficult when I have to trust what others are seeing in the distance. Especially when they are teenagers. And my Corvette gets stolen.

Who Stole My Corvette?

I was such a car nut. My current obsession was a prized 1969 "Bad to the Bone" low-slung, sexy white, Corvette Stingray with a .... oh wait, I was starting a story about my WIFE's car. I had bought her a car that only showed off her beauty as its driver. It was a 1984 C4 Corvette, the first fully redesigned Corvette in 15 years. It was built with a Doug Nash "4+3" transmission - a 4-speed manual coupled to an automatic overdrive on the top three gears that went 0-60 mph way too fast.

For my bride and me, our big decision at the time was the move to Hawaii. Once we knew it was a sign from God, we pushed anxiety out of the way. We were finally able to let ourselves get excited. We set about the tasks of leaving. Our driving force was the hope and promise of the blessings and prosperity our Heavenly Father had prepared for us. Everything went pretty smooth and easy until it came to dealing with a certain candy-apple red Corvette.

The car was a Valentine gift to my lovely bride, customized from the front bumper all the way to the taillights. I chose the paint to match my favorite color of fingernail polish on her, (OPI's "I'm Not A Waitress") - That meant it was Candy-Apple Red and faded to Candy Brandywine on the rocker panels.

It suited her personality so well that is was only fitting the license plates read 4MYWYF. Unfortunately, the Corvette was not going to be accompanying us to Hawaii. We needed to get out from under the debt and sell it to make a clean start (along with our house, the work truck, the "Bad to the Bone" Vette, and most of our possessions).

Not surprisingly, we found a buyer quickly. Right before our move to Hawaii, I drove the car to the buyer's office building to deliver it to him. He was a lawyer and his office was the entire top floor of a prominent bank building in downtown Phoenix. I arrived after business hours, so I was not surprised to see hardly anyone around in his large, lavish office.

We had settled on a pretty straight-forward deal. I was to collect the sizable down-payment via a personal check and the balance was to be wired to my bank account the following week. During our meeting, he had asked me to sign over the car title.

But I was no dummy, I told him I would not sign over the title until I had my money in full in my account. He seemed to find that reasonable but wanted a contract to that effect to protect his interest. I thought that sounded reasonable. He had a notary standing by, so after the signatures we shook hands and he assured me the balance would be wired to my account.

We talked amicably as he drove me home that evening. I even took the opportunity to share the Lord with him. I stood in front of my house and watched him drive away - I felt good. All was well and I was leaving in the morning.

The next day, my bride and I headed for Hawaii with all the gusto of new found freedom - the big adventure had begun! We set out to enjoy our first weekend there, determined to unwind and let loose of all the stresses and pressures we had just been through – we had made it!

Life was so good!

On Monday, the process of settling into a new life began. The business with the Corvette hung in the back of my mind all day. Then I got notification from my bank that "Larry's" check had bounced. No way was I waiting for the wire to come through. I called his number several times and there was no answer.

I called my dad in Arizona and asked him to go to this guy's office and see if he could confront the guy. Being a good sport, my dad agreed (dad was also the co-signer on my car note so he had an interest in this).

When I made the initial deal with the buyer, I made it clear to him if I didn't receive the wire I would report the car stolen to the police. I figured that since no title had changed hands, I had it covered.

My heart sank when my dad called a few hours later to tell me the news. At the top floor of the same bank building I had been to just days before, my dad found the entire suite empty. I was dumbfounded and confirmed the address twice with him. Yep, the guy's name was still on the door but not a stick of furniture or a soul inside. All I could say over and over was, "YOU'RE KIDDING???!"

Anxious to get to the bottom of this, I gathered the only information I had on the guy, a photocopy of his check, and began making calls. My first call was to his bank branch in California. After one of the tellers told me that "Larry" was one of their most colorful customers and she knew exactly who I was talking about. She even commented about his flashy new ride.

Great! I had him. I identified myself as the owner of that red Corvette. The teller said, "That is the most beautiful car I've ever seen." I said, "It's stolen." The teller claimed she didn't know anything about that, but repeated, "It's one of the nicest cars I've ever seen."

I repeated a little louder this time, "IT'S STOLEN." This was going nowhere; it was time to call the police. I dialed the number with all the confidence in the world that this was the right solution and I "had him" now – justice would be served and this would soon be over.

Believe it or not, I was wrong on all accounts. After explaining it several times to different officers I understood my blunder. If the guy had just taken off with the car, it would have been theft. My downfall was that I signed a CONTRACT with the guy and had it notarized.

Do you understand?

In the eyes of the law, this guy and I had an agreement. I handed him the keys voluntarily and he failed to uphold his end of the bargain. My only recourse? Sue him. That's it. All I had was a civil case.

Legally, he had not stolen the car at all. It was unbelievable to me that I had fallen for this hook, line and sinker. I thought I had been thorough, when in actuality – I had been played.

According to the law, there was nothing the police could or would do. They were not going after him or the car. I was sitting in Hawaii literally thinking, "I have just given my car away."

I didn't think it was possible to add to my frustration level, but that was tested when my bank called me. Apparently, they needed a car payment from me because I had not paid the note since leaving for Hawaii.

I explained the car had been stolen. When they asked for

the police report number, I tried to explain but they were not into any complicated explanations. Great. I was still liable for the car and the car payment.

My anger quickly boiled to the surface. "What if we don't pay it?" They responded, "We will send out the repo men to re-possess it". What? That was a great idea. I even had the car's whereabouts.

Next was the easiest most gratifying answer I could think of in the heat of that moment, "I have a location it was seen at a few days ago. If you can find it, you can have it. Now, go get it!!"

My frustration was way over the top. I couldn't get anyone to help me. The police wouldn't help, the teller wouldn't help, my bank wouldn't help, and at the bottom of all this was the deception! I was very distraught.

My Corvette' was stolen and hadn't been found. The move to Hawaii had added to the rising debt we had and now I had to pay off a stolen car? Not knowing what to do felt like I was in a hole with no way to climb out. Moving to Hawaii was supposed to be like starting over. Life was new and here I was reaching back trying to get some of the old. "What do I do God?"

We spoke to family and friends in Arizona pretty often during this time. As leaders of a large youth group, we had left behind lots of familiar faces. One of most favorite activities, a summer weekend in LA with the youth, was coming up and we weren't going to be there. We had talked of flying back so we could lead the teens on one last adventure but the looming stolen 'Vette's debt was killing us.

In one such conversation, we lamented to our youth group about the car being stolen. The kids, all 50 of them, pledged "WE'RE GONNA FIND YOUR CAR!" Wow, what a squint towards the future. We didn't see it.

Their gesture of boldness made us smile so we agreed, "Sure you will!" The more we talked about it, the more adamant they got, "God is going to move and we're going to find your car." Kids have x-ray vision sometimes, but we still weren't seeing it.

Knowing they were serious we tried to downplay it and cautioned them to keep out of harm's way. We encouraged them to call the authorities instead of taking the law into their own hands if they actually even saw the car. They prayed about it and asked God to let them be the ones that found that Vette.

In a time when these teenagers were displaying such incredible faith, our belief was that the car was long gone – it was history. It had probably made its way to some chop shop in Mexico, never to be seen or found again.

Several weeks passed and as the end of the summer neared, it was time for the youth group to go to California for the annual "Sing by the Sea" conference.

This event was hosted by Pacific Christian College for church youth groups in the southwest. Every summer the kids would stay on campus for a weekend of fellowship, fun and games. There would be a whole day at the beach with bonfires and concerts, and the weekend would end by going to Magic Mountain on Sunday afternoon.

We had made that trip with the youth group three years running – the kids just loved it. This year, our great friends, Paula and Paula, would be taking the group. Friday afternoon came and three 15-passenger vans loaded down with kids and cargo left Arizona for the all night drive to California.

All were excited for the power weekend ahead. Paul, one of my best friends, was driving the lead van. Ricky, who was riding shotgun, was my disciple. Ricky had taken his girl, Maria, to the prom in that Corvette and was one of the most vocal about wanting to find it.

As the miles and hours rolled by, the laughter and chatter dwindled as darkness came and the van was soon quiet. It was a moonless night cloaking the road and everything around it in total darkness. All anyone could see was what the headlights touched.

Around 1:00 a.m., monotony had set in and Ricky was keeping Paul awake by playing the Tail Lights Game. It was a game the guys would play by guessing what kind of car it was based on its taillights.

Paul and Ricky had been talking about nothing when Ricky looked up ahead and saw the reflection of taillights and said "Yeah, that's a Vette, I can tell by the round taillights." Paul squinted as if it magnified his vision and continued to stare out of the windshield into the darkness.

As they got closer, the car appeared to be moving pretty slowly. Yes, it was a Corvette alright. Closer still, they realized it wasn't moving at all. In fact, it was parked over on the side of the road. Paul was going about 55 mph when they drove by it and for that split-second their headlights hit the license plate.

They saw "4 MY WYF" clearly as if it had been boldly and intentionally illuminated. They looked at each other immediately, eyes wide with recognition, and said in unison, "THAT'S ROB'S CAR!"

Brake lights burned brightly as they immediately veered off the road and screeched to a stop. As each van approached, the recognition hit and they immediately pulled over.

This dark stretch of highway was flooded by light as doors flew open and everyone spilled out of the vans and ran towards the car. Paul and Ricky were the first to reach the car and took another long look at the license plate. The kids began to jump up and down and shouted, "WE FOUND IT!"

Several thousand miles away our phone rang and I answered; it was Paul. All I could hear was the kids screaming "WE FOUND IT! WE FOUND THE CAR!"

While Ricky tried to calm them down, Paul's voice came yelling over the phone, "You're never going to believe this; we are standing by your Corvette!" I wasn't sure I heard him right, so I motioned to my wife to come and listen. With our heads together he repeated, slower this time to pronounce each word carefully, "WE_FOUND_THE_CAR!"

Paul explained as they were all parked on the side of a deserted highway in California in the middle of nowhere. Our entire youth group had the car surrounded in a victory dance shouting, "WE FOUND IT."

Do you understand the significance? Just like they had squinted and ALREADY SEEN... they, ALL together, ALL at one time, found our car. What were the odds?

We asked if he was sure it was our car and we could hear the amazed disbelief in his voice as he both laughed and cried the answer, "Of course! It still has your license plates on it." Unbelievable!

From this point, things happened quickly. Half the youth group appointed themselves guardians over the car (because if the thieves came back, they weren't getting the car back).

The other half of the group went to the next town to notify the Sheriff, who contacted the repo man to take it back to Arizona.

In the days that followed, the bank checked the car out and told us it was still in mint condition. In fact, there wasn't anything wrong with it other than it was out of gas. We summarized the thief had run out of gas and left it sitting on the side of the road, who knows how long ago or for how long. It was eventually sold to satisfy the debt at auction and we were off the hook.

We also found out that Paul and Ricky had taken a short-cut off the main road that night. They weren't completely lost, they knew they were heading west and would eventually come upon the main road again, but they were not on the road they had planned to be on that night. Somehow they had ended up on that backwoods, deserted trail of a highway on their way through California.

I ask you - what were the odds of the entire youth group actually finding the car? Three vans filled with our youth group, unexpectedly turn onto the very deserted highway where our stolen car had run out of gas. Who would have ever thought that?

Then... they ALL found my car, ALL at once, ALL together. Who would have ever thought that? It was a miracle!

When the kids said, "We will find your car," it was their child-like faith that God heard, not mine. I am a man of faith, but I did not have the faith that they would find the car. My weak eyesight could not squint that far.

My faith had said, "Not even just one of them will ever see that car again. It is gone, gone, gone." But the fact that they, the ENTIRE youth group, would collectively ever find the car was ridiculous. It was impossible to know that.

Since that was impossible, it was exactly the arena God was most excited to show His glory. He doesn't just show off, He gives a story to pass down through the ages.

This is a staple story in the Moore household; we've told our kids this story many times over the years. They have heard us tell it to our friends, new believers, unbelievers, and skeptics.

It is a well worn tale of God's amazing divine authority. It was a day that God put a series of unimaginable circumstances together that produced the Corvette miracle.

The story was solidified years later when one of our youth group kids came to visit us in Texas. Ben, now a man in his 40's, gladly told the story to my own kids. Hearing it from someone who was actually there that night spoke to them in a way my version couldn't.

Ben told them what it was like to see the car and then actually touch it. It was a defining moment in his young life to witness such an event. When he paused, we all knew that night was about much more than just finding the car.

It was a connecting point to God in his young life that he still hung on to today. Ben continued, "It was a miracle." That was the simple truth.

Today when I ask God to intervene in my insignificant life, I ask him for more. He is the God of the Impossible and He has shown me what it is like to get MORE than I ever asked for or even imagined. I pray often to have "eyes to see." It requires a squint of faith.

My motive is not to get a miracle, it is to allow my God to show off. He wants to demonstrate His authority and power in the lives of those who will have child-like, impossible-believing faith. What are you squinting for today?

Believe for MORE. Squint harder. See farther.

For my own life, I believe my Maverick Mentor wants me to move forward, not to wallow in the struggles, but to strive ahead to the future He holds for me. There are people who don't have any clue about the things I struggle with because I choose to live in the future. I don't see myself as disabled, handicapped or limited. I see myself as who I will be. I don't know exactly what the future holds, but I do know **who** holds the future and I do know He loves me and has an excellent plan laid out for me. There was one time I thought my future was very short. I was being swept out to sea on the Molokai Express.

Molokai Express

While in Hawaii, I was scuba diving with a new friend, Bryan. We were both considered "haoles" or "foreigners" to the locals because we had not been born and raised in the islands. This day happened to be one of those picture-perfect days that tourist's fall in love with – the Hawaiian sun high in the sky, bathing warmth on my skin as we walked to the sandy beach. Today, I was a dive instructor about to take Bryan out for his advanced diving certification. We were surrounded by a tropical paradise of white sand, lush green vegetation and the sun reflecting off the ocean water as we performed our pre-dive check.

Once done, with gear in hand, we walked out into the water a few yards before stopping to put on our fins. I looked up at the big blue sky again and said a silent prayer before I put on my mask. I gave Bryan the "okay" sign and he gave me one back – we were ready to go.

We descended into a silent, beautiful world of tranquility. Even though Bryan was less than ten feet away at all times, it was easy to feel small and alone in the ocean depths. This world of incredible peace was alive with teams of colorful fish that swam around us as we descended. Beams of sunlight filtered by clear ocean water hit the coral reefs, commanding them to come alive with vivid and brilliant colors. The only sound I heard was my own breathing.

At about sixty feet we came across a bunch of fishing gear; lures, hooks, weights and such. Being a fisherman, Bryan couldn't resist grabbing this treasure, and with my help, we quickly collected enough to realize the weight of it would affect our dive. We set it in a well-marked rocky outcropping and headed for deeper water to continue the certification. As we swam along the contour of the ocean floor, I watched as the gauges marked 70 feet, 80 feet, 90 feet. As the Dive Instructor, it was my job to monitor and watch Bryan closely. For his certification, we had to go down beyond 100' so that was our shelf for the day.

We were at depth, so I had watched the clock and our air supply carefully and now it was time to go up. In our ascent we kept an eye out for the treasure we had set aside earlier, but we hadn't spotted it yet. Relentlessly, Bryan searched for our ocean booty and was very determined to find it. I found myself swimming after him, caught up in a frenzy to find his stuff. We had looked for a long time and our air supply was getting dangerously low, so I grabbed hold of Bryan and signaled to him we had to go up. When we surfaced, we realized our quest for the treasure had led us far away from the safety of the protected dive cove. The lures had lured us out further than planned, just like in my vision. Anxious to swim back in to safety, we felt the pull of the current and realized we had been caught in the Molokai Express – this was bad.

The Molokai Express is a current that pulls at its maximum strength between Oahu and the island of Molokai. This Molokai (Kaiwi) Channel is approximately 26 miles and known for its unforgiving conditions; unpredictable wind and strong current and surf. I could see a beach. I could see the water's edge. But the current was pulling against the swells and swimming in was an option that was disappearing fast. We needed to make a push and give it everything we had! I was a very fit, strong swimmer and so was Bryan. Our eyes connected for a second, silently communicating what we had to do. The idea to swim back was going to take a lot of work. So we flipped over on our backs and started kicking like crazy to get ourselves out of the current.

We swam side by side and fought hard for any forward progress for over thirty minutes and only got about fifty feet. That was how strong the current was. While we swam, we talked to each other, we prayed together, we did what we could to keep each other calm. The power of the moving water was gargantuan. To try to outmuscle it was to risk exhaustion and death, but if we stopped in this current, we would lose everything we gained. Another 15 minutes passed and I went into my realistic mode. We had to face the fact that we had not made any real progress. We were both nearing complete exhaustion. Desperately, I considered dropping our weight belts, but no, we couldn't do that or we would have been like bobbers bouncing around the middle of the ocean on top of the waves. So we doggedly kept swimming even though we could no longer see the beach. The only land we could now see was a cliff with a shore break into razor-sharp rocks. If either of us panicked, we were both done. I contemplated what our next move should be – stop swimming and be carried over to the rocky cliff? The water was crashing against the coral rock and that would kill us. What do we do? We were even more tired and we had kept each other calm, but we both knew what the outcome was most likely going to be – we were going to die there.

I imagined we looked like two tiny specks in the vast ocean, with miles of nothing in sight and no hope to hold on to. It is often said that when the end is near, one sees their life flash before their eyes. For me, I thought about my beautiful bride and my young son. I was just so tired of swimming. I thought about just turning over on my stomach to breathe in a bunch of water and just let go. There was no way I would survive this. Finally, I did turn over on my stomach, not to give up but to scan the horizon again. There was nothing but water forever on one side and cliffs on the other side. We couldn't go anywhere. We'd been in the current now for over an hour. Bryan and I locked arms and began to pray again; loudly. The fear was no longer hidden as we were both on the edge of sanity and fighting to stay afloat. We pulled out every Scripture we had ever known and prayed it back to God.

Mixed in the sound of our voices shouting out our prayers, I heard a new sound. I turned to look and out of nowhere a boat appeared, not more than 100 yards away. It was a small fishing boat and I could see a weathered local man onboard. I wasn't sure he could see our two tiny heads bobbing in the water or if he could even hear us at this distance, yet he was coming straight at us. Just minutes before, when I had scanned the horizon, there was no one. I was very sure that my Maverick Mentor had sent that man in the boat. How was it that I hadn't seen nor heard the boat approach? Sound travels faster under water than on land. What happened next was very surreal. I watched as the boat got closer, moving as if in slow motion. In my mind, I had gone so far deep into thinking I wasn't going to make it that I was having trouble understanding what I was seeing. I SEE A MAN AND A BOAT!! Is this real or is my mind playing a trick on me in my last moments? Is all this just happening in my head? All I could hear was my heartbeat as it thudded in my ears, but it was soon drowned out by the sound of the approaching motor.

The man was close enough now; I could see a deep frown on his face as he leaned over the side of the boat. He gestured with hands poised above his head signaling "Are you okay?" We both immediately responded by frantically waving our arms over our heads signaled (and shouted) "NO, WE NEED HELP!!" He glided smoothly near us and with seemingly little effort, literally plucked us out of the water and out of the Express. WE WERE SAVED!! Bryan and I stumbled weakly to the floor of the boat. Lying there, exhausted and panting, I looked up at the beautiful Hawaiian sun and I repeating to myself I'm alive, I'm alive, I'M ALIVE and I'm going to see my wife and son again! "WE MADE IT!" A mere second ago, all was hopeless and now all is right again! I cannot describe the relief I felt as I praised God, while the boat chugged along.

Within minutes, the fisherman's boat took us around and into the cove and to the sandy beach where we had started. The man eased the boat into shallow water then Bryan and I jumped in to the calm water and we easily swam the short distance to the beach. As soon as we got to the beach, we each collapsed finally letting out the pent-up emotions of the reality we had just experienced, knowing how close we had come between life and death. We were simultaneously laughing and crying. I cannot explain to you all the things that ran through my mind, but I know my life was saved that day. It was a defining moment for me. A man in a boat appeared just seconds before we could have perished.

Bryan and I sat on the beach then, laughing and praising God saying, "Can you believe that?!!" We prayed for each other, for the man, for our families that we would soon see, and for our Heavenly Father who had sent a man and a boat to save us. As we gathered our gear and walked away from the beach that day, my thoughts were filled with plans to hug my wife and son, longer and harder than ever before. Because I was saved, I had a future and would see my son grow up!

I will forever be grateful to the man in the boat. I'll never forget the look on his face as we thanked him for saving us. The hat over his sun-weathered face did not hide the wisdom I saw in this sea fisherman's eyes as he slightly shook his head in dismay. As the boat pulled away, I read the writing on the back of his boat, "A Hui Hou" – that will be forever etched in my mind. Although he didn't say it, I knew he was thinking "You haoles don't know the ocean." And he was right. But we do know the God that made the oceans. Thank you, God, for rescuing me!

People don't always see their futures come to pass in real life, but this time I did. After I was rescued and I was lying in the boat trying to catch my breath, I knew it was God that saved my life. It was like He came out into the miry clay and set my feet upon the rock. It reaffirmed to me that He has a plan for Rob Moore here on Earth. The plan was not to perish that day. My future was in his hands.

Faith gives us the ability to see beyond what is natural to what is SUPER-natural. This is very important for a defensive position. Satan continually bombards us, but if our squint can see those missiles coming, a wedge will not be driven between the Savior and the saved. It is also a great collective weapon, used to protect others, as we band together and strengthen each other with our faith. It gives us a hope for the future. We become an unstoppable force of unity. It is God's future for us.

My faith is a mighty shield. It can deflect even the most

vicious attacks without transferring the full force of the assault to my soul. Satan is always heaving fiery darts of worry, fear and doubt in our direction but I let my shield of faith take the blows. Ultimately, I believe God is in control; that He is working everything for my good; that what happens is for the best of everyone involved. However, He reminds me that my shield can even knock my opponent backwards and incapacitate the enemy. When Christ was being tempted in the desert by Satan, His faith in the Word of God repelled the deceiver. God tells us that our faith cannot be just in our minds but must also produce actions of obedience and serving. That's what gives the enemy a good shove backwards.

There was one time when my best friend was losing everything he loved, but the Lord had a great future for him. My squint towards the horizon gave me a mighty vision that took TWELVE years to come to pass, but it punched the enemy in the gut every time worry, fear and doubt surfaced.

Patience, Prophecy and Friendship

Patience is not one of my virtues. I am a "git 'er done" type of person who doesn't sit around and hope and wait. But I have discovered in my life that there are some things that take time. Two come to mind...prophecy and friendship. This story has both.

It's a rare gift to have a genuine friendship – at least it's a rare gift for me. I mean it's really hard to have a depth of relationship because it takes a lot of time and effort for men to get there. It's a powerful thing to get to know someone, gain a life-long friendship and an understanding that I never expected to have. That's what Michael Valentino is to me – a true best friend; we're spirit brothers from a different mother. We have hit many of life's crossroads together where we've locked arms in prayer for each other and our families. I am going to tell you a story that began with a prophecy and carried our friendship for over a decade.

We met in our early 20's, while attending the same church in Arizona. When introduced to Michael I remember thinking, "This is someone I should get to know."

To be honest, that was a very foreign thought to me and not usually one I would follow through on. Michael took the initiative, and one day after church, asked if I would help him lay sod in his backyard.

That afternoon, two acquaintances from church got together to work, and through the course of the afternoon, discovered similarities in life and all things spiritual. We were young, in construction, and deeply devoted to our Father. That was the day we became kindred spirits.

Over time, as our friendship grew, it became easier to share life. It gave me comfort to know I had a friend I could talk to about anything. We became thick as thieves and together, with our wives, we all became best friends doing life together.

It was a great day when Michael told us they were expecting a child. **HALLELUJAH!** For as long as we had known them, they had been trying to get pregnant, so this was very welcome and very exciting news! We knew they had experienced a lot of difficulty and had gone through desperate measures to conceive. The emotional toll this journey had taken them through had them believing they could not handle any more disappointment.

During this time, my lovely bride and I had news of our own. We accepted an opportunity of a life-time and it meant we would be moving to Hawaii! Over the next couple of months, it

was a very happy time for each of us as we prepared for
the future we believed was a gift from God and our divine path.

The afternoon of our going away pool-party, it was
controlled chaos at our house which was over-flowing with well-
wishers having a great time. Everybody from church was there –
except Michael and his wife. As our best friends, we knew there
is no way they would miss this, so after a while I called him. At
the sound of his voice, I immediately knew something was
terribly wrong. In a controlled, but deeply sadden voice, he
explained he had been at the hospital because his wife had
miscarried. They had lost the baby.

There was no way to describe the feelings we went
through. I mean there we were having our BIG going away
party celebrating our new future in Hawaii, while our best
friends had just lost their last hope for a child. It was so hard, so
emotionally difficult to comprehend. We wanted to be with our
friends. Immediately after the party my wife and I went over to
see them.

On the drive over, my wife cautioned me that it's not the
right time for us to say anything, because we ourselves had never
been through anything like this. She advised me there was
nothing I could say that would make it better. Let's just listen and
hold their hands she said. Agreed? Of course I agreed – what
would I say?

We arrived at their house and I immediately saw
Michael standing on the driveway, bent over with his head under
the hood of his car. My wife went inside the house and I walked
up to him. He stood up to greet me and I just grabbed him and
wrapped my arms around him. I held my best friend as he let his
emotions go. He cried and I cried. I really don't know which of
us was holding the other up, but I'd like to think it was me being

strong for my friend who had just lost his child, his baby.

I had never felt somebody else's pain like that. He could barely speak, his voice full of emotion. Tears streaming down his face, he explained she had miscarried there at home. It was gut-wrenching to hear the agony he and his wife had gone through that afternoon. I listened to him cry and I was speechless. I couldn't help but think to myself, "Why did this happen?"

Eventually we went inside and the four of us sat in their living room, talking and weeping together. My wife and I tried to be comforting as much as friends can be in a time like this. It was getting very late and we decided to pray together before leaving. The four of us were sitting on the floor, holding hands with heads bowed and my wife prayed first, followed by Michael and his wife. They prayed kind of tight-throated. Emotions were very raw and they were trying hard not to breakdown again. It was my turn to pray and just before I started to speak, the Lord gave me a picture – I saw it but I heard God say, SPEAK IT. With my eyes closed I spoke aloud. . .

"I'm standing in front of a carousel and Michael you are there standing there next to me. We're both looking at this carousel – it's a carousel of horses and there are several kids riding it. (I pause with recognition). THEY'RE OUR KIDS Michael, yours and mine – I SEE IT so clearly, I SEE IT!!!"

To have this vision of such intense joy at a moment heavy with despair can only be God sent. It was so beyond comprehension! The picture of Michael and me standing there watching our children riding the carousel together! OUR KIDS! I was so overwhelmed with joy that I could hardly keep it in. In my excitement I realized my wife was squeezing my hand, trying to shut me up.

She whispered in my ear, "Please don't give them false hope; they don't need this right now." Michael was holding his wife and she had her head down, not looking at me. I looked at my best friend and said with tears, "I'm sorry, I didn't mean to overstep." It must have been painful for them to hear my vision. It was very quiet in the room, as no one moved or said anything.

My wife had stopped squeezing my hand, but she was still holding it, and it felt comforting. I looked at my friend again, and when he looked back at me I knew without saying anything that Michael got it - he understood what had just happened. In a time of turmoil, God had given us a glimpse, a prophetic picture, of a precious promise. Michael's response was a simple, "I receive that."

Fast forward several years ahead and life had brought some changes. My bride and I were settled in Hawaii and were now a family with two of our four kids born. The distance between Arizona and Hawaii had not deterred our friendship with Michael, as we heard from him often. He and his wife were no longer married. Simply put, sadness had filled their lives past the point of recovery and they divorced. Michael was going through a really long time of hurt and brokenness grieving for the relationship. We were happy when he decided to come to Hawaii and stay with us for a while. He needed some time to heal; to get away from everything and get a fresh start.

On the day of his arrival we took him to church with us. As we walked in, a pretty young woman (stranger) walked up to Michael, put a flowered lei over his head, kissed his cheek and said "Turn the page." Michael only had time to register surprise, before another pretty young woman walked up and did the same thing. Michael laughed as one after another came up from every direction and repeated the process until he had lei's stacked up to the top of his ears. (Little did he know, a certain friend of his had put them up to it).

Each time they said, "Turn the page." The way I saw it was that he had suffered a lot of loss and I was trying to help him get over it. He needed to see that he was at the end of a chapter in his life, so he had to turn the page to start the next chapter. Life was new. It's a new start.

Having Michael around was good for all of us. Our two young children loved their Uncle Michael – he was their party king and biggest fan.

Whether it was hearing my son laugh and scream as he and Uncle Michael "washed" the car (Michael allowed himself to be squirted by the hose continually by a hysterical 3 year old) or seeing him toss our baby girl high in the air while she squealed for, "MORE! MORE!" and covered his face with kisses, it was clear to me that God saw his heart for fathering.

Watching him play with my kids and be a presence in their lives never failed to remind me of that prophetic vision from years before. Once, I had asked him privately if he remembered the vision. With no hesitation he replied, "I remember it very clearly and I hold on to it." We fell silent after that, each of us not having to say what we were both thinking. The vision was getting away from us – with each passing year it seemed more unlikely to figure out how God would be able to work out something like that.

Michael stayed with us for about a year, but it was clear from the beginning, his plan was to return to Arizona and move on with his life. When he did, he was on fire to get back, get a place of his own, and go back to school. He planned to keep his head down and his nose to the grindstone until he got his degree.

He called me one day with the news he'd heard his ex-wife had remarried. I recognized this tone in his voice. There was more to the story. He continued by saying she had been pregnant and recently gave birth to healthy twins; both had gone full term. He was crushed all over again. Their dreams had come true for her. For her, everything was great and her life was moving on. Yet, my prophecy specifically had Michael in it and – well, it was just not happening - YET.

Michael is a deeply spiritual guy and even with this news of his ex-wife, he trusted his faith to tell him, "You just don't see it yet." I encouraged my friend to stay the course and do what he was supposed to do, let the Lord work things out. Michael had decided he didn't want to date – he was done. Do you know the phrase "famous last words?"

Out of the blue, one day he calls and explains that a friend of a friend wanted to set him up on a blind date. I knew Michael HATED blind dates and never ever accepted them. I smiled to myself as he continued to voice his protest about it over the phone.

Finally he ended with "I don't want to go." I said, "Don't go."

Despite his handsomeness and his suave ways, he was a man of character who really didn't want to do the wrong thing. He didn't want to be that guy who thought he was too good to do this. His friend had told him that she was a single mom with kids and he thought she could really use a break and go out for a nice dinner. Michael said, "I just feel like I need to be a good Christian guy and do her a favor." He didn't want to feel bad by saying no, but his heart just wasn't in it. He said yes.

He called me on the drive home from the experience and said emphatically, "I had a divine moment." I listened while he told me the story from the beginning.

Turned out that his blind date lived two hours north of the city, so his plan was to drive up to her town and take her out to a nice dinner and then drive the two hours back. On the drive up there, he was listening to worship music just passing the time in the car and the spirit of God hit him hard. He cried so hard and was so overcome that he was concerned he would crash the car. He pulled the car over and asked God, "What's going on?"

The Lord said, "Don't mess with her, she's my daughter. Don't play games with her, this is not a game."

Michael took notice – he thought he was just doing her a favor by taking her out and God just corrected him, "HEY this is not a game!" They met and Michael took her out on a simple picnic – minus the kids. She did not want her kids to meet a "blind date." He said he really felt like something miraculous was happening. He felt like the Lord said he should marry her. "WHOA!! What?"

"Last week this was a mercy date, you just met this girl and now you're going to marry her?

SLOW DOWN COWBOY!"

I thought, "He's leaping from being single to being a married man with three children." Since Michael had not dated since his divorce, I was convinced he wasn't thinking straight. Yet here he was, having all of these spiritual connections. I heartily cautioned him to take it slow. Still, I could hear the seriousness in my long-time friends' voice. "The Lord told me I can't tell her my intentions until she asks me what my intentions are."

I was thinking, "Praise the Lord!" That's good news, because I figure it will be a LONG time before that happens.

Two weeks go by and Michael was chomping at the bit –
literally. She introduced him to her kids and he loved them. He
kept telling me how amazing this woman was and how she's got
the Spirit of God on her. He was so crazy excited! Each day
they were calling each other and falling head over heels for each
other.

So finally came the day when she said to him, "Michael
Valentino, EXACTLY what are your intentions with me? This is
not a game to me, I've got kids." She was calling him out. They
were the words he had been waiting for.

Michael replied, "It is my intention to be your husband
and to be the father of your children."

She didn't expect that answer. The relationship
snowballed into hyper-drive after that. Three months from their
first date, they were married. We flew in from Hawaii to be part
of this amazing union and meet Michael's new bride and
family. Taking on a woman and someone else's kids never was
in Michael's game plan. What he got was an amazing strong
Christian woman that surrounded him with a loving family. It
was really divine the way God put it all together.

Fast forward again and life went on. Michael was a big
player in the hotel business in Arizona and he was flying all over
the country making sales. He had such an outstanding year that
he received a promotion and was given an opportunity to write
his own ticket. They told him he could choose to be Sales
Manager at any of their hotels he wanted. The chain had just
acquired a luxury hotel in Maui, so he chose to return to Hawaii.
He packed up his family lock, stock and barrel for the big move
to the spectacular Grand Wailea Resort.

My bride and I were very happy that Michael and his
new wife were going to be close by and we excitedly got ready

to receive them. They were going to fly through Oahu on the way to Maui and spend an overnight with us. We hadn't had much of a chance to visit since the wedding and were looking forward to just getting together and letting the kids play. When they arrived, it was clear the long plane ride and managing three kids had worn out Michael's wife. My own bride had a migraine and was bravely trying to fight her way through it.

Michael and I decided to take the kids out and let our wives stay at home to get some downtime and rest. So we all scampered off, me and my kids and Michael with his three kids. We unloaded into Chuck E Cheese and the kids ran off to play. Michael and I settled into a booth to relax, have a drink, and just catch up on life. About two hours went by and we decided it was time to go find the kids and go home.

We walked into the gaming area, eyes searching for any one of the seven. We were immediately surrounded by brightly colored balloons, games with multicolor lights and the screams of children having fun. For a moment, not one of our kids was in sight. But as my eyes swept the room, I stopped dead in my tracks in awe. As I turned my head to see Michael's face, I confirmed Michael had the same jaw-dropped look of comprehension. Simultaneously, we pointed in the same direction and said, "THAT'S INCREDIBLE!"

Across the room, in our line of sight was a merry-go-round, a carousel of musical horses. The horses looked magical, their poses prancing as if dancing as they moved up and down and round and round. Perched atop the horses were all four of my kids and all three of his kids. They squealed and called out to us and waved at us each time they rode by. "Daddy watch me!" "Can we stay longer?" "Look, I got on all by myself!"

This was it. This was THE PICTURE in the vision I had

12 years before we had kids. All of our kids, HIS kids and MY kids, were all piled together on that carousel of horses just like I had seen it on that dreadful empty night so many years before. What had been just a flicker of hope for so many years had just BURST into flames. God was so true. The picture came to life.

Michael and I both just collapsed in laughter and tears of happiness spilling down our faces. I slapped Michael on the back as he pointed to the children and said "No way!" Time did not move as we just stood there and marveled at the beauty of it all. We really saw it come to pass, years upon years later; it was exactly how I saw it. It was really divine the way God put it all together.

In this story, it seemed for such a long time that there was really no hope or no way that God could fulfill what He had spoken through the prophecy He gave me that night. When He did fulfill it and speak it, it was right on time and absolutely with the right people. It's real and believable because we saw God do it . This is a big long story and it's very cool. It's true and real. I adore my friend for allowing me to live it with him. I was able to squint far into the future and shield him with my faith in Jesus.

We live in this Burger King society where, "I want it my way and I want it now." But when we step back and we say, "I'm doing it your way Father, in your time Father," that's when we can have a whole different atmosphere of life. Our faith gets built by what we hear. And I believe our faith gets expanded by what we see.

The future is not in my hand. Actually, I never even think about it because God controls it and He loves me, I'm His kid. Right now, in the physical struggles I'm currently going through, I can look at this prophecy coming to fruition. It helps me live right now with patience for the vision I've been given for my future healing and the prophecy God has given me for my future. It taught me to hold on tight. It taught me to hold on long. It taught me to have patience in prophecy and friendships. It gives me the ability to hope and to wait. That is a virtue in itself.

As it says in Jeremiah 29:11 - " For I know the plans I have for you," declares the Lord, "plans to prosper you and not to harm you, plans to give you a future and a hope. **Even if you have to squint, know WHO holds your future.** This is **lesson five** of my Maverick Mentor.

Round Up Questions:

1.) Without change, where is your future headed?

2.) What are you hoping for in your future? Do you see any evidence of it?

3.) What has the world (or your parents) taught you that you need to unlearn so that you might have child-like faith?

4.) Is there a vision or a dream that God has given you?

5.) Who holds your future? What is the plan for you? Where do you see yourself in five years?

ROB and ROBIN MOORE

CHAPTER 7

"Changing Hats"

It is a defining piece of attire. It distinguishes the wearer from a distance. It is an item of apparel that can be worn in any corner of the world and immediately identifies you with North American cowboy culture.   It is the cowboy hat.

I have never known anyone who "found" a cowboy hat. You can find Yankees ball caps, football helmets in stadiums or even on airplanes. You can even find a sombrero or two at Goodwill. Not cowboy hats. They are usually taken or acquired, not found.

You've seen it happen. A guy puts on the hat one of three ways: (1) Hat tipped back with a howdy-folks, aw-shucks grin; (2) Hat brim at eyebrows with a Clint Eastwood squint or; (3) Hat pulled down to make a scowl with a ready-to-draw arm wave.

Wanna play cowboy? Just get the hat. There is an awesome power that cowboy hats have on the wearer. Just put one on and there is an immediate and dramatic transformation.

I will never forget the famous "Hat Duel" in *For a Few Dollars More*. Clint Eastwood as the "Man With No Name" goes toe to toe with Lee Van Cleef, "The Man in Black" - Colonel Douglas Mortimer. The two bounty hunters are after the same prey (the villain Il Indio) and were bound to meet up at some time. Clint tries to run Mortimer out of town and they have a chest bumping, boot scuffing, pissing contest like two little boys. Clint finally punches Mortimer and dislodges his hat. As Mortimer tries to pick up his hat, Clint draws his six gun and shoots the hat several more feet away. With each attempt Mortimer makes to pick up the hat, Clint's expert marksmanship keeps pegging the hat farther away. Finally, Mortimer and the hat are far enough away that Clint misses. Mortimer replaces the hat on his head and he draws his weapon. In a stunning display of prowess, Mortimer not only shoots Clint's hat clean off his head, but each successive bullet keeps it tossing in the air like a seasoned juggler. Clint's wide-eyed look of respect is priceless.

Director Sergio Leone said of Clint Eastwood, "As an actor, he has two expressions: with and without the hat." Any which way he wears it, the hat makes the man.

My Lord has some cool headgear as well. In Isaiah 59:17, it says that He bears a chest plate (like my fringed jacket) and there is something upon His head that bears salvation. Like a cowboy hat, it is front and center for all to see and distinguishes him from all others.

Our salvation hat is like that too. It protects the head, where all thought and knowledge reside. Jesus Christ said to me, "If you hold to my teaching, you are really my disciple. Then you will know the truth, and the truth will set you free." (John 8:31-32, NIV) The truth of salvation through Christ does indeed set me free.

Unfortunately, those who reject God's plan of salvation battle Satan unprotected and suffer the fatal blow of hell. 1 Corinthians 2:16 tells me that believers "have the mind of Christ." Even more interesting, 2 Corinthians 10:5 explains that those who are in Christ have divine power to "demolish arguments and every stronghold that sets itself up against the knowledge of God, and we take captive every thought to make it obedient to Christ." (NIV). Now that I wear this hat, it is amazing how great I think it will look on everyone else.

I remember when my iconic salvation cowboy hat was annoying to my dad, but there is a time when he donned a hat of his own.

We all have the ability to choose whose footsteps we will follow in this life. But, it is a little unnerving to think that someone will someday look up to you and want to follow in your footsteps. It gives you a moment to pause and consider what tracks you are making.

"Making the Incredible From the Impossible" was the motto for my Phoenix construction company. Even today as I read it, I see so much of my father in it. Both my Heavenly Father and my earthly father. The roots of that phrase can be traced to the three generations of custom builders in my family. My dad taught me everything I know; as did his father before him. I worked with my dad until my late teens.

In the beginning I was just the little kid hanging around his father while he worked, but I took to it and he helped me develop solid skills that set the course for my future. That was the kind of dad Stan Moore was. When I started my own company, it was a no brainer to ask my retired dad to come to work for me. I was a son following his father's footsteps and it was a joy to have him close by me.

My dad came to my house every morning so we could ride to work together. He would sit down and have a cup of coffee while he waited for me. On this particular day, while waiting, he noticed some poster boards that were leaning against the wall in the kitchen and began to casually read them. The day before, my lovely bride and I had our church youth group over for a day of prayer and fasting. We had written our prayer requests on these poster boards to pray over them and ask God to answer them. I had forgotten to put them up. Right there at the top of the list was his name. He had zeroed in on the line that read 'I pray that Stan and Katy Moore would find salvation through Jesus Christ.' That was obviously my request. His boy was putting his "un-Christian-ness" out there for everyone to see. Not only didn't he like it; in fact, I found out later that it really bent him out of shape.

My wife and I had been saved for about three years at this point. We were very on fire in our walk with God and were in a church that taught us to pray boldly and step out. My parents saw the turn our lives took. Since they had grown up in a quiet Methodist tradition, the Assemblies of God intensity didn't sit so well with them. Certainly, they were convinced we had been sucked into a cult of some sort and that we were brainwashed. We let them see who we were in Christ and didn't hide our newfound spirituality from them. If our devotion to attending Sunday services wasn't enough, we also went to a mid-week service and Bible study. All family events had to be scheduled around our church activities because that was our priority. That drove them nuts. This spiritual vitality was so foreign to them that they viewed us as being overboard, obsessive and obviously: "Jesus freaks." (I say if you gotta be somebody's freak, I choose Jesus every time).

My dad let me know that seeing his name written on the poster board was bringing him into this "whole thing with your church – into all of that cult stuff." He waved his hands in the air to signify the largeness of what "all this" was. He thought it was way over the top and I had gone too far. My salvation hat was seen from a distance by him and it jangled his nerves. From my view, this was nothing new. It was everyday life for me; he knew that and I thought he accepted it.

I don't know, maybe he thought he was now on a "target list" for the church people to round him up and rope him in. In a sense, it was true. He had a large target on his back now...a prayer target. God is a pretty true marksman and after we placed that bulls-eye on him and my mom, we got faithful in our prayers.

He saw that faithfulness every day at lunch when I prayed over our meal before eating. He would politely wait for me to pray before opening his lunch. This was my normal that he thought was so abnormal. I loved him for being honest.

After some time off between jobs, it was back to the daily grind for me and dad. On this particular morning in my quiet time before leaving for work, I asked Jesus to come into the conversation via my father. We hadn't talked in a while and I was praying that I would find a new way to broach the subject of salvation. Instead of me being the one to bring it up and wear it, I wanted it to be my dad who asked to try it on. I just didn't want it to be like it always was: I would bring it up, and he would change the subject.

That afternoon at lunch, after I said grace over the meal, my dad said, "Son, I've got to tell you something." We worked together so what he had to say could have been about anything.

I replied, "What is it, dad?" From across the table, he said "Your mom and I found something that you found a long time ago."

I thought, hmmm what did I leave at their house? Were they cleaning out some storage space and came across some of my things? Curious, I asked him, "What did you find, dad?"

What he said I will repeat verbatim here, because I will never forget it. He said "Only the love, the peace and the joy that Jesus Christ brings." I sat there stunned with my jaw on the floor. (He didn't find the cowboy hat, he picked out one for himself!)

Ignoring my hanging jaw, he continued, "The bottom-line is, today we don't think you are a Jesus freak. We have been going to church every Sunday for over a month, and in fact, we're considering also going to church on Wednesday nights."

I had a flow of questions that welled up in me and I peppered him. When? How? Why? I didn't even know he was shopping for a cowboy hat of salvation. For whatever reason, they were reconnecting spiritually.

Well, I am pretty sure it was because the whole element of praying for somebody, instead of preaching at them, hit the bulls-eye. I couldn't wait to tell our youth group that they just literally prayed them into the Kingdom! Praise our precious Lord and Savior. God had plans for my parents!

Fast forward a few years and the picture changed considerably. My parents became very sold out for the Lord. My dad read the Bible and often called to ask me questions. There were times we would pray together too; yes it was a very different picture. My dad had health problems, most of them being heart issues to the degree that he was in and out of the hospital.

The issues compounded and went on for years. Throughout, in his good humor, my dad would refer to it as a rollercoaster ride. One day he was healthy and riding high and the next he would decline and go back to the hospital. For years, even after I moved to Hawaii, the doctors would tell my mom and I that dad was "touch and go" and that we were going to lose him. This went on for 20 years – yes, I'd say God had plans for Stan Moore.

From the time I was a young boy, he and I always had this way of being in the same room without speaking but we could still communicate. Whenever he was in the hospital, I would go and sit with him. It was an amazing connection I had with him to sit and not say anything and we did this so many times. It was such a rare gift.

I remember seeing a photograph someone took of us during one of these moments. There we were, a mirror image of each other. We both had the same posture, the same placement of hands, same legs crossed and with the same look of concentration on our faces.

Once, it was just the two of us in his hospital room one day. There is no script for going through a time like this with a loved one. It's hard to know what you should do/not do or what to say/not say, so you go with your heart. I leaned over and kissed him on the lips, which is something I had wanted to do for a long time just to let him know that I really cared and that I really loved him.

He remained quiet, but I could see by the way he looked at me that he completely understood my intent and totally received it. I asked him if he was scared. He looked at me with clear eyes and said "There are three of us in this game," he continued. "One is me and I'm going to do everything I can to be successful." "The doctor is two and he's going to do everything he can to be successful." He paused and looked at me with such intensity that I got the message that he truly believed what he was about to say. He said "then there's God and He WILL do everything that is successful."

My dad eventually went home to be with Jesus many years later, but this is not a story of sorrow, it's a full-on story of HOPE. Because I understand now that I actually didn't lose anything. I actually gained something because now I KNOW he's at home with Christ. That day when he talked about Christ, he spoke with a passion that finally matched my own.

I understood it was something he had to say - an accumulation of what he wanted me to know. His hat was well worn by that time. The sweat of his brow had etched the band of the hat as he prayed about things he couldn't change. His salvation was real to him because he felt the kiss of heaven with every labored breath. Because of that I know there will be a day when I will see him again. Oh, we still have our way of communicating. Sometimes I talk to him and I feel like he hears me; or even that he tells me hey I'm thinking about you. I know he truly is in a much better place and he's setting up a space for me.

When I think about my dad and our time together, I'm extremely grateful for him being my dad and for teaching me the way he did. It may sound odd, but the silent communication made our bond stronger – it was not things left unsaid, in fact it was things that didn't require saying because there were no words to describe it. It was cowboy code. I started out with the intent of tying this up as a great story about a son following in his father's footsteps to ride the trail of life. Because I cowboy'ed up first, my dad followed in my trail of salvation. Now that the story has been told, I can clearly see that wasn't the case at all. My dad did follow in his father's trail, his Heavenly Father - the Creator of the Universe who saved him. Yes, I'm happy to be riding that trail as well.

There are few other items that you can wear that carry the same iconic weight as the cowboy hat. "Never wear another man's hat, ride his horse or sleep with his woman," as the saying goes. It is the stuff of legend, the dares to do the dangerous, the risk a cowboy is willing to take once he knows his salvation or who he is really riding for here on earth.

There is one other cowboy who goads the maverick in me. His salvation is as secure as my own and he wears the cowboy hat cockily. Let me tell you about what we saw one day down in the streets of south Phoenix...

Truth or Dare in South Phoenix

The pulse of his heartbeat was loud in his head. He was blinking back the sweat that was dripping into his eyes as he was keeping a lookout. It was another hot day in Phoenix and here he was again, standing on this downtown busy street corner.

He did his best to throw out some swagger, but he was fooling no one other than himself. He was nobody doing nothing and going nowhere.

"God, help me. Let this be the last time I have to do this. I want a different life."

The car came again. It was the second time that exact car had driven by, so it must be time.

THUMP. THUMP. THUMP. His heart pounded louder and faster the closer the car got. He looked for the usual gestures and then moved into position as the car approached the third time. As he took a step off the curb, there was suddenly an explosion of light. He staggered back, blinded for a second, trying to get his focus.

"What was that? Was it a reflection off a building?"

Slowly his vision returned to normal . As he looked around, everything appeared to be the same, except it wasn't. He had forgotten about the car which was now gone. Confused he looked again for the source of the piercing flash and the reason for this sudden feeling of change.

Then he saw them. They were coming toward him, two men, covered in light.....

Cowboys will be cowboys. My buddy Michael and I are no exception. We enjoy a good-natured, yet competitive game of one-upping each other. It's how cowboys rib each other. We especially like to challenge each other in our boldness for Christ. It wasn't so much "Who would do it better," as much as it was, "Would you do it or not?" It was kind of like a game of spiritual Truth or Dare. Not backing down is the only way to win at Truth or Dare.

Years ago, while living in Hawaii I would make routine trips to Arizona. It was a given that Michael and I would get together. On this visit, we decided on a day of golfing. We set out dressed-to-kill in our golf attire. I couldn't say much about Michael's outfit without risking ridicule of my own. We were stylin' men ready to get LOUD out on the course.

The weather was perfect and we were having a great time. As we neared the 18th hole, Michael not so nonchalantly tells me he has a whole box of Bibles in his car.

"Are you game to go pass them out?" he challenged.

I could see the glint in my friends' eyes and they were not from the bright sun. He definitely had thrown down the gauntlet. I could hear that trilling whistle from the spaghetti western in my head. Daaaa-daa-da.

"Of course," I said, "Let's go right now!"

The challenge was on! We continued the banter as we walked out to his car. We had our swagger on. Each confident that the other was going to take it up a level. We got to the car and Michael nodded toward the open box. I saw the stack of Bibles – maybe 25 in all.

"Where should we go?" Michael asked innocently.

I took the bait. "Well, South Phoenix of course," I responded with a huge smile.

"Great," he said, "No need to change clothes, let's go as is."

Without skipping a beat, I replied "Exactly. Why change clothes?"

Okay, so dare it is. Neither of us said anything as we rounded the car and got in, but we were both thinking the same thing.

South Phoenix was the last place two upper eastside boys should be; let alone two upper eastside boys wearing golf clothes. But I didn't back out and neither did Michael. Game on. Cowboys will be cowboys.

Turning on to Van Buren Street was sobering. The buildings, fences and storefronts were dominated by spray-painted monotones of black, gray and white, depicting rage and gang life. Because of the shadows cast by the towering buildings, the area was devoid of sunlight. It was dark and gloomy like the mood of the people on the street. It was like looking at a black and white photograph with no life.

Yes, there was the usual hustle and bustle of a busy downtown thoroughfare, but there were so many people that sat lifeless in doorways, bus shelters or leaning against the walls. I was struck by the fact that no one looked me in the eye. Yes, this was the right place for Michael and I.

We headed for St. Vincent DePaul's Food Bank. Although it was in a very bad part of town we also knew it was a place of hope for some very down and out folks.

Truth or Dare #1

Once inside the food bank, it was a very different world. The colorful walls were adorned with simple murals painted in bright vibrant colors. They depicted families of all ethnicities united as one community. One people under God – Amen!

We walked into a large open room where many were seated at tables having an early dinner. We walked over to the food line and asked if we could speak to the manager. Almost immediately a tall man with a weathered face and keen brown eyes appeared. We introduced ourselves and explained we'd like to pass out some Bibles.

"It's against policy," Steve said. He explained the rules against passing out religious materials. Michael and I looked at each other. We're both thinking this is St. Vincent's right? – I mean isn't this a religious organization?

While we were scratching our heads, Steve came from around the counter and quietly said, "I'm leaving for 20 minutes and when I get back, I don't want to see you here." His manner was abrupt and his movements exact as he removed and folded his apron - but his voice was not. "I will be gone for exactly 20 minutes," he repeated looking directly at us with a knowing wink.

We did not miss the spark of humor in his eyes as he smiled and said, "Do you understand what I am saying?"

Without waiting for a reply, he walked away. We got the implied message. We wasted no time in going around the room and handing out Bibles to the seated diners. Mavericks.

With each Bible there was a quick conversation, a handshake or a smile as we moved among the people there. I couldn't help but wonder how God was going to use this. Before the twenty minutes were up we were outside again and we each had one Bible left.

(SCORE: TEAM JESUS = 1, ENEMY = 0)

God directed our attention to a young man standing on the corner. He was anxious, agitated, looking around and sweating. We were intrigued and were compelled to head in his direction.

Truth or Dare #2

Then he stepped off the curb and staggered a bit. He blinked several times and looked around as if in a daze. I couldn't help but notice he was staring right at us as we approached (maybe it was our golf attire?) – He stared at us oddly as if he saw something we couldn't.

Once we reached him, he seemed very interested in

talking to us and we sensed he was hungry for the Lord. In the 10 minutes or so that we spoke to him, we noticed a car that would pull up across the street, idle there for a minute then pull away. By this time, the young man didn't seem to notice the car at all. He told us about wanting to get off the streets and into a better life. His eyes never wavered once we started talking to him about Jesus. He listened intently and seemed to absorb every word we spoke and readily accepted our offer of prayer and Michael's Bible. The truth transformed him and answered his prayer right there on the sidewalk. Another cowboy added to the trail ride. Hope had sprung up in him as he hurried off.

(SCORE: TEAM JESUS = 2, ENEMY = 0)

As we turned away, a middle age man followed behind us. Seemingly disoriented and distraught, he spoke to us in broken English, From what we gathered, he was "visiting" the area (illegally?) and gotten separated from his family for the last three days.

Truth or Dare #3

With no money, no food and no transportation, Julio had ended up at the homeless shelter. We gave him our last Bible and told him the good news of the Gospel. He gratefully accepted our offer to pray together. We joined hands right there on the corner and began to pray aloud. We prayed for his soul, the city and the regrouping of his lost family. He was weeping. He was like a little lost sheep.

Before we could say, "Amen!" Julio shrieked in Spanish. Then, he burst into a long torrent of excited screaming and pointing. There was a van coming our way. It was Julio's family! They piled out of the van and smothered him with shouting, hugs and giant gestures. We could understand Julio explaining our presence there on the corner and the name of Jesus being praised. After many "Gracias, senor!", the family loaded back up with Julio in the shotgun seat and drove away.

Michael and I grinned at each other. Jesus was going 3 for 3 with us today.

(MICHAEL, ROB & JESUS = 3, ENEMY = 0) Kingdom advantage. This bull was whipped.

How often do you get to be a part of changing someone's eternity? Any day on the golf course with my best friend is better than a day at work, right? But Michael and I are Kingdom men. Advancing God's Kingdom is our primary leisure activity. We don't schedule time to advance His Kingdom, we do it because that's WHO we are.

TRUTH: God has a great plan for someone's life but allows you to share this good news with them.

DARE: Believe the impossible and get out of your own way to allow God to work through you.

Truth or Dare? It is more exciting than any game of golf. Cowboy up!

Why is salvation marked by head gear? The head is where all our thought and knowledge reside. The truth sets us free (John 8:21-32).

1 Corinthians 2:16 tells us that believers "have the mind of Christ." Even more interesting, 2 Corinthians 10:5 explains that those who are in Christ have divine power to "demolish arguments and every pretension that sets itself up against the knowledge of God, and we take captive every thought to make it obedient to Christ." (NIV) The Helmet of Salvation protects our thoughts and minds and is a crucial piece of protection.

There is one time I had need of head protection to ward off the blows of Satan. He was swinging doubt and discouragement, trying to direct my attention to Reality. He was pointing to my failures, my sins, my unresolved problems, my health and every negative thing you could think of in my life. He wanted me to take off my hat and lose my confidence in the love and care of my Heavenly Father. He wanted me to lack hope in the future promise of salvation and entrance into heaven. My Maverick Mentor changed my thinking by taking me back to a time of remembering what He had done in the past for others, to give me hope for the future.

Looking Up

It often happens that my life and travels take me through my treasured Arizona, my home-state. It's a place where I have roots and just breathing in the warm air feeds my soul. While there, I can always count on my good buddy Michael to chauffer me to and from the airport and around town. It's our thing – a routine two long-time friends enjoy. We have a special bond, much like brothers do. We go from finishing each other's sentences, to taking communion together, to charging up our internal competitiveness. Yes, we're just like brothers. It's a powerful gift to ask a friend "do this" knowing that he would.

Today Michael and I are at the Phoenix airport, sitting and waiting for the flight that will take me back home to Hawaii and to my family. Continuing our routine, we pray together before boarding.

We begin by asking that God would allow me to sit next to somebody with whom I could share Christ. This prayer is very intentional – we WANT me to meet someone. Our next prayer is for me to be able to NOT sit by a single woman on the hours long flight. I feel like it honors my wife not to sit with single-women when I'm traveling alone. My flight is called and passengers move by unnoticed by us as we sit facing each other, eyes closed and heads bowed in prayer. Amen.

Feeling energized and equipped, I board the plane. For me, the thrill is not anxiety or fear of who I'll sit with but the purpose and certainty of what lies ahead of me. It's not because I'm on a trip; it's about having a captive audience for the next 5 or so hours. I can make a huge and lasting impact in someone's life and I WILL do this, so let the games begin! I find my seat and sit down next to a young woman who is sobbing. I ask what the matter is and between sobs she explains that she's newly married and her husband is sitting at the back of the plane. Without hesitation, I offered her husband my seat. I didn't mind. As it happens, this same situation presents itself again, and I good naturedly exchange seats 2-3 more times knowing that I am a pawn in God's chess game on this flight. All this good will has me in good spirits, but a little disoriented like a fast paced game of musical chairs. I'm standing in the aisle when I hear "sit down." I turn toward the voice and see a woman pointing to the aisle seat and she commandingly repeats "Sit down! I'm a flight attendant and we hate it when you guys don't sit down so we can get moving. When we get up in the air, you can find another seat if you want." Under the circumstances, I could have given it more consideration, but she was adamant and I decided okay. God had a plan.

The One

All is quiet as the crew guides the big jumbo DC 10 through a smooth take off. The passengers begin to settle in and the would-be flight attendant introduces herself as Karen. Behind her practiced casual manner and smile, I sense something else. We chat casually back and forth. I learned she was on vacation with a girlfriend, who was seated across the aisle from me.

Sitting between the two, I thought about switching seats. I don't sit with single-women and she's exactly the one I wouldn't and shouldn't sit next to. She was young and very pretty – there was worldliness about her. But I knew it wasn't about me at this point. God had a plan.

It wasn't long before our conversation turned toward God and Jesus. I told her stories of the miraculous that I had experienced. It was not enough for me just to experience the transformational salvation of Jesus Christ, I wanted everyone to experience it.

I shared with her the love Christ has for His people. She listened quietly as I shared my story. I could tell she was intrigued and impressed that I was so solid with what I knew. She said she really wanted to believe, but it was just so far-fetched. She said, "You have no idea who I am – I have a lot of baggage."

For the next few hours, we discussed her baggage. She was so much of the world, having travelled abroad and lived by habits procured along the way. Through the hours, I dispelled her baggage.

She would say, "What about this one, what about that one?"

I said, "God can take care of that."

Through all her hurt and temptation, God gave me the words I needed to share Him and dispel her past. I had her full attention, so much so that as the flight attendant served my beverage; Karen intercepted it and placed it in front of me on the tray.

I said, "If I could say right now IN THE NAME OF

JESUS for this cup to disappear and it went 'poof' and it disappeared, would you believe?"

She said, "Absolutely!"

Then I said "I will pray for you every day for the next week while you are in Hawaii, that you will see a much bigger miracle than this cup disappearing."

She smiled and I knew a decision had been made. That day high in the majestic blue sky over the Pacific Ocean, Karen accepted the Lord.

The afternoon rolled along and I thought of the hours of conversation I had just witnessed. The peace pulled my thoughts towards my waiting family. My wife makes me a photo album every time I travel. I love carrying it with me because it reminds of the happiness I feel as a husband and father. I felt the need to show Karen the pictures of my wife and kids and our happy life together.

We came to a picture of my brother of choice, Michael, with my kids and Karen said "Wow, who is that?" I smiled and explained it was my buddy Michael. "Is he single?" she asked. At this particular time, he was.

How many times in my life had a woman asked me that about Michael? Aside from being my best friend, Michael is also quite handsome. He can date anybody he wants, no problem. Women flock to him. Karen would be flying back through Phoenix the following week on her return to LA, she had a full day layover – would I set her up with Michael?

I explained that he only dates Christian girls. She cheerfully responded, "I accepted Jesus; I'm a Christian girl, aren't I?

I knew he would do it if I asked him, but should I ask him? I agreed to set it up and she gave me a phone number where she could be reached.

Shortly thereafter, we landed in Hawaii. I was struck with the overwhelming gratitude of being home and ready to see my family. Karen waved to me as we departed. The next day, I called to tell her I had set things up with Michael and that my wife and I would like to bring her a Bible. We set a time to meet in the hotel lobby. She received her first Bible.

God Had a Plan

A week later, while on a layover flying through Phoenix, Karen met Michael as promised. I heard from Michael shortly after their visit. He spoke of the time they spent together and how incredible the revelations were.

They ended up in Starbucks having coffee talking late into the afternoon. Karen told of how I said I would pray for a week that she would see a bigger miracle than a cup disappearing. "I haven't seen it," she said.

Undeterred and smiling, Michael replied, "I see it, do you want me to tell you?"

She responded, "Absolutely."

Michael spoke, "First, Rob doesn't sit next to single-women on airplanes. He honors his wife and he absolutely won't do it, period. But, he did when he met you because he sensed God had a plan for you. The two of you spent a few hours talking about God, and about the miraculous that he had experienced. Second, you accepted the Lord Jesus Christ on the airplane, which is a miracle in itself. Third, did you know he was in a car accident on the way to the hotel to bring you the

Bible?"

She shook her head slowly that she was not aware, tears starting to form in her eyes. Michael continued, "Lastly, how many days did you read the Bible last week?"

She replied, "Every day."

"Now", he said, "before you came to Hawaii to meet your girlfriends, if somebody would have told you that you're going to talk to some random guy for four hours on the airplane about God, accept Jesus into your heart and read the Bible every day of your Hawaiian vacation, would you have believed them?"

She laughed and said no way-not a chance. "In addition to all that," Michael said, "you have a blind date with me. – I DON'T DO BLIND DATES - EVER, but because it was Rob, I agreed to – do you know why?"

There was no reply, just silence. "Because I prayed with him about YOU before he got on the airplane that day – God had a plan. The bottom line is, THESE are the miracles that I see and the easiest one being that 10 days ago, would you have ever seen that you lived the life that you've lived the last seven days?"

Tears exploded from her eyes as she tried to speak, "I see it! I see the miracle now and it is greater than the cup disappearing."

Fast Forward

The next five years brought big life changes for me. I answered a calling that my family embraces. Yours truly became a Pastor of a small church. No surprise there. I felt like I'd been doing it one way or another for a long time.

Two years into it, I felt like I was coming to a point where I had to stop and ask myself if I'm really even making a difference. "Do I have anything to offer?" I was beginning to think maybe I heard Him wrong. I had witnessed epic growth in our church and then epic decrease, more growth then more decrease. "What if I went back to doing what I was doing before? Would anyone even ever notice that I'm not pastoring anymore?" I've always been good at knowing no matter where I am, there is where I'm supposed to be. I just didn't feel like I was doing anything that made a lasting impact into the eternal. In all honesty, I was doubting.

None of this escaped my wife's notice. Truth be told, she saw it way before I ever sensed it. Every day, she'd say "You go, honey!" or "You're doing a great job!"

"Thank you God for giving me my solace in her presence, she is my biggest cheerleader." As loving as her encouragement was, it was like your mom telling you you're beautiful. You're like, "DUH! Of course, you think I'm beautiful, you're my mom." I appreciated her encouragement, but it didn't penetrate. This did not stop her and I couldn't stop how I felt either.

My Wife Tells The Story from Here

Rob went off to work one day and I prayed to the Lord. "I don't know what else to do. I don't know how to do this. I've reached the end of me. Father, you need to do something from your side to encourage him to continue to do this, because I can feel it, he's ready to quit. It's just not working out for him. I am ready to leave in your hands to encourage him in a way that only you can. In a way that he knows beyond a shadow of a doubt that you made him for such a time as this."

So, that day he comes home early, it's about 3pm in the

afternoon, and he goes straight to bed. I ask him if he's sick. He gives me a depressed NO - I just want this day to be over. Grasping, I say, "Hey you got some mail; want to go through the mail?" I was desperate for anything to perk him up. I pull out a card from the stack, "Hey, look you've got a card!"

There was no indication of who it was from written on the outside and it was nowhere near his birthday. I'm thinking maybe somebody has written him a nice card saying 'good job" or something. I look at him and he doesn't even care. I asked if I could open it. I was a little curious, "Who is writing Rob a letter?"

He replied, "I don't care, you go ahead." He was firmly in his funk. I decided I was going to read it out loud to him, so I pulled the letter out and read...

Dear Rob,

You must be wondering who I am. About 5 years ago, I was your seat mate on an ATA flight bound for Hawaii. I was on a vacation with a girlfriend of mine (we were both flight attendants for US Airways) and you were giving us some friendly advice on what to do there. Not long after take-off, you and I got into a wonderful conversation about religion, Jesus Christ, and the Bible.

Oh, what little I knew then! If you recall, I didn't even know the Bible was divided into 2 parts – the Old and New Testaments. I also wasn't aware what it meant "to receive Christ" or to have a personal relationship with God. You told me of your love for Christ and what He has done in your life. I was captivated while you shared your encounter with the homeless man and your experience with your first building project. I will forever remember that flight and our talk.

I would like to tell you of the incredible journey I've been on since we met. When I returned from Hawaii, I had a strong desire to learn about the Bible. That, however, only lasted just a few weeks. It seemed quite overwhelming so I decided to put it on the back burner with the hope that someday I would pursue it further. That "someday" finally came about 2 years later when I went in search for a church and found one I connected with. Throughout that next year, I had what I now know to be God tugging on my heartstrings to go deeper. I attended a few Bible studies, a retreat, and had several talks with my pastor and other spiritual leaders about my hunger for the Lord and the desire to feel Him in my life.

I prayed that same prayer that you led me in several times in the following two and a half years, and I still felt as though God was not there. At that point, I could not yet bring myself to say I was a Christian because I didn't have that peace, joy and love for the Lord that I saw in other Christians. There was a void deep within. I just knew there had to be more, and with that in mind, I was persistent and set out to search Him with my whole heart.

Finally, last June, after 3 years of really searching, I was truly blessed when I ran into Katrina, an acquaintance from work, I remember being drawn to her sprit; she glowed when she spoke of God. I wanted what she had. She had given her number to me, but I was apprehensive about calling her since so much time had passed. I decided that if I were to run into her, I'd take that as a sign from the Lord. Two days later, I not only ran into her, but she was on 3 flights of mine. I am absolutely positive that God's hand was in the meeting. Through His grace, I have come a long way. Katrina and I have been reading and studying the Bible in depth, starting with Genesis, and we are now in the book of Isaiah. She is quite knowledgeable in His Word. God truly is working through her to minister to me and to others as well. She has been such a blessing and a great inspiration, and I thank

God for Katrina. It wasn't until I began reading God's Word on a consistent basis that He revealed Himself to me. I now have the most incredible relationship with my heavenly Father. I really never knew what true faith was or how wonderful life could be. I sure know now.

I've thought about that ATA flight many times since and wanted to write to you. I'm sure you had given me your name and address, which I had apparently lost. God knew my desire and answered my prayer. The other day I was witnessing to a friend of mine who had questions about a one-year Bible. I found the one you had given me, and as I opened it, there was your name and phone number. I rejoiced when I saw it, and even more so when I found through the internet that it appeared to be current. I can only pray that you will in fact receive this letter and it finds you well.

I believe that God puts certain people in one's life for a purpose. God used you to plant the seed which laid dormant for a while, and then He used Katrina as the sun and rain to help the seed sprout and grow. I know I have a long way to go, as we all do, however, I now realize that as long as I remain in Him, He will continually keep pruning so that I can blossom into the person that He intended me to be. Through my studies, I have found that the Bible is like a mirror, for when I look deep inside the Scriptures, I see my imperfection staring back and strive to become more Christ-like.

I would enjoy hearing from you and what you've been involved with these past years. You had a profound impact on me and I'd like to stay in touch. God's blessings to you and your family.

Yours in Christ,
Karen

As I peeked during my letter reading, I could see the tears rolling down his cheeks. You don't think he perked up? What an amazing sense of renewal! It was like life itself was breathed back into his spirit.

Now, I was weeping. "God, not only did you bring this letter today, but of all the days she could have sent it and it could have been weeks ago. But to have it sent so it would get here on this day, at this moment which was amazing in and of itself." It was my turn to feel my spirit breathed back into me for the answer to my prayer.

Backtracking, my mind whirred. Wait! God sat him next to her on that airplane five years prior knowing that she would then write a letter which five years in the future would be the very thing he needed to lift him up. THAT IS MAGNIFICENT!

We just see this little bit like one piece of time. We think of salvation as "sit next to this lady so she'll get saved." We don't see time the way God does, the circle where it comes around in 5 years. That moment in time when it's going to inspire you to keep going when you don't think that there's anything left. Or you don't think it matters. It was totally amazing to me, that was the beauty of it. I didn't have to do a thing. It wasn't my work to do. I wasn't even thinking of it that day. "Oh God, help this day."

God started working on this project 5 years ago or even more. Because she had to think about going to Hawaii, she had to make that plan to go, so when did that bug get planted in her mind? When you realize the complexity, it's so beyond what we could ever think of – so beyond.

That's the amazing story about the girl and how she donned her cowboy hat of salvation. She learned about the Lord, slid back, got brought about by another person and then was hooked.

For me, God's plan began with the call of ATA Flight 79 and a prayer to keep me out of an awkward situation, to a time of confusion where I could not hear, to remembering that we're all just a moment away from where we're meant to be – in Christ. The encouragement is you really don't know what you say, or how much water it holds for tomorrow. You're in a rodeo every day but it lasts for eternity.

There was a moment in time that I literally had no time to think. A guy was on the ride of his life on a runaway horse. I only had minutes to secure his hat.

Suicide Option

At this time I was the Project Manager of a church campus and all its buildings in Kaneohe, Hawaii. The church's property sits on 12 acres of lush, beautiful land atop a steeply sloped mountain hillside with panoramic ocean views. It was just another day in God's paradise. I was inside the church building, getting a drink from the water cooler and I could hear Annie, the church secretary, on the phone. I waved at her as I walked by, but when she saw me she began to frantically wave me over. Holding her hand over the phone and before I could speak she said, "Here's Pastor Rob!" and handed me the phone. Pastor Rob? I wasn't a pastor (yet). Feeling a little off guard, I raised the phone to my ear to say hello and heard a voice say "I'm going to commit suicide; I'm going to kill myself."

My thoughts raced – "What do I say? What do I do?" Mentored by a Maverick whispered in my ear, "Rob! Get a hold of that hat before you do anything else."

My first sentence to him was, "How serious are

you?" He told me it was a "done deal." The maverick in me said aloud, "Really? So you are going to kill yourself. Okay then, I only have one question for you: When you wake up, where will you be? In heaven or in hell?" There was silence on the other end of the line.

He shouted, "Are you crazy? I tell you I'm going to kill myself and that's what you say?"

Unfazed, I reply quietly, "I'm more concerned with where you will live in eternity, than I am with your temporary situation at the moment."

Silence again. I knew I had him thinking. I needed to stall him while Annie picked up another line to phone the Honolulu Police Department. Good girl. I knew they would track him down if I could just keep him on the line.

He began to talk non-stop. As he recounted his tale of marital heartbreak, he began to get emotional. He was still defiant, but his boldness had subdued. I could now hear uncertainty in his voice. He revealed his name was Tony. Sensing that the tables had turned toward me, I began to ask him a series of leading questions. I was able to get enough information out of him to find out where he was calling from. I quickly wrote out the details and handed them to Annie and she passed them on to the authorities.

Okay folks, it's time to ask the big question. What happened to make him want to take his own life? The emotion in his voice was thick as he explained it was his third wedding anniversary and that he and his wife had recently learned they were expecting their first child. They had planned this trip to Hawaii as a special celebration. At dinner the night before she dropped the big bomb. His wife told him she was actually pregnant with his best friends' baby, that she no longer loved him, and that she was leaving him for the other guy. Some friend. Tony was devastated. He left the hotel that night and wandered the streets of Waikiki for hours. He needed time to think. Finally able to cope, he decided it was time to try and discuss things with his wife so he returned to the hotel. He arrived to find that she had checked out and had taken his bags, his airline tickets and all of their money – leaving him with only the clothes on his back and $9.00 in his wallet. His attitude seemed to have shifted now that he had told his story. He began to listen more and talk less as I spoke encouragement over him. Then all of a sudden he cursed at me and the phone sounded as if it had been dropped. The next voice I heard was that of HPD Officer Kamai asking me who I was.

A week later while back on the job at the church property, a phone call comes in for a "Pastor Rob." Annie knew just who to look for. I was summoned to the office for a call that was waiting. I was surprised to hear it was Tony. "Hey, you remember me?" His voice started out hopped up with attitude.

He was clearly mad. "Because you called the cops, I had to spend the last week in a psychiatric ward!" Sensing I wasn't going to get a thank you, I changed the course of conversation and asked how he was. His tone changed, "Man, I don't know. They're going to release me from here tomorrow." Pressing in, I asked him why he chose to call me of all people? He replied, "I don't know anybody. I have no place to go and no money to get back to the Mainland. I don't know what to do – can you help me?" Prodding a little further, I asked about his "reflective time-out" in the psychiatric ward. He admitted that he started off hating my guts but the week of thinking about my question, "Where will you wake up?" had really burned into him. "I guess the real reason I wanted to call you, Pastor Rob, is because you seemed to have something I wanted. You had an assurance about your future that I didn't."

Aha, now I had Mentored by a Maverick moment. Tony's eternity was about to be secured by Jesus Christ. I could just feel it.

Time to trust God and watch Him move. It was time to involve the body of Christ for every one of us to experience His presence. At the time, I was leading a small group or as our congregation called it: a "mini-church." When our mini-church met that night, I filled them in about Tony and sat back to watch what God would prompt in their hearts. They had prayed for this lost soul the week before when he was just the "suicide jumper." Now he had a name and a story. Immediately, things started to work together as the group made plans on how to help Tony. Daryl, who had been a resident at the same mental health center after his wife left him (coincidence or God-incidence?) offered to pick Tony up for his journey home. He felt he would have a connection and a comfort level with him like none other. Brent, who was also working on the job site at the church property with me asked Daryl to bring Tony by the church after he picked him up so he could give him a personally inscribed new Bible and show him around. After taking up a cash collection for Tony, I asked Daryl to bring him by my cafe for a little sit-down on the way to the airport. What I didn't realize is that Daryl would be bringing Tony into his family home where his elderly mom fed them and washed Tony's week old stinky clothes so he could fly back to Texas all fresh and clean. Peggy, who worked for Hawaiian airlines, got him a gift of a buddy pass for a direct flight home and Kai, who was a waiter at one of the most upscale Waikiki restaurants, footed the bill. A prayer warrior couple, Aaron and Anita, waited at the airport to give him his airline ticket and lay hands on him to encourage and strengthen him for his journey yet to come. Tony was going to be surrounded by people being the hands and feet of Jesus all day. God had it all under control with a part for everyone to play.

It was time. As I met Tony at the cafe in the middle of this masterful orchestration of people from his trip to the psych ward to the airport, he appeared to be in awe of what he had received thus far. When I gave him the envelope with the monetary gift collected for him, gratitude was clearly on his face. Tony was so amazed at the outpouring of love by all these people he had never met. "Here I am, a total unknown," he said. "Why are perfect strangers going out of their way? Why would they care so much?"

I shared that is the love of Jesus and the Hawaiian thing - Aloha of the Holy Spirit. He was perplexed. I explained the "Aloha" is a combination of two words. "Alo" means to transfer or to share and "Ha" is the Breath of Life. "Aloha" means to share the breath of life. (That is why it can mean, "hello", "goodbye" or "love"). I watched as the pain in his face turned into a smile of redemption.

"I WANT THAT" he said. Right then and there I had the incredible privilege to introduce him to my Maverick Mentor. Jesus is the very breath of life! (Genesis 2:7, Job 33:4, Isaiah 42:5)

Tony's very own new Bible showed him the way as I walked him down that old Roman Road...

Romans 3:23 All have sinned and fallen short of the glory of God...

Romans 5:8 God demonstrates His love for us that while we were still sinners, Christ died for us....

Romans 6:23 For the wages of sin is death but the GIFT of God is eternal life in Christ Jesus our Lord.

Romans 10:9-11 if you confess with your mouth, "Jesus

is Lord," and believe in your heart that God raised Him from the dead, you will be saved.

It was so awesome to see the intense joy in his eyes as he asked Jesus into his heart. He was glad to be ALIVE and was looking toward the future and leaving the past behind. As he said goodbye and drove off to the airport with Daryl, I could see how God used a suicide as the option to lead a person to saving their soul. I realized that although he moved on with his life, every time I drive past that property, its God-print and his story are etched forever in my memory.

Even though I do not understand why, I truly know there is a spiritual reason behind the struggles and challenges I have personally faced. God's sovereignty rules over my time here on earth. There is a reason that the enemy has not been able to take me out in a frontal assault even though he has tried. He hasn't been successful in depressing me with the self-pity sucker play either, as I deal with my disabilities. All those close calls have done only one thing: make me very determined in my salvation.

Like a cowboy hat transforms the wearer, salvation transforms the soul. **Not only will I have a transformational salvation experience, I want to see others transformed by changing hats.** That is **lesson six** of my Maverick Mentor.

Round Up Questions:

1.) Do you own a cowboy hat? How did you get it?

2.) What has been your biggest transformation moment?

3.) How have you cowboy'ed-up and left a trail of transformation for others to follow?

4.) How have you partnered with the transformation of someone else?

5.) At the end of this life's journey, where will you wake up for eternity? Do you want to change that? (If you don't know how to be sure where that is, see the last pages of this book.)

ROB and ROBIN MOORE

CHAPTER 8

"Wield Your Weapon"

Clint Eastwood as Blondie: "You see, in this world there's two kinds of people, my friend: Those with loaded guns and those who dig. You dig."

My own observation in life: "There are three kinds of men: The ones that learn by reading. The few who learn by observation. The rest of them have to pee on the electric fence."

I try hard to be one of the first two guys, learning by observation and carrying a loaded gun. My Maverick Mentor taught me early that the Word of God would be my six gun, but I had to read it. It was my offensive weapon to strike against the enemy and just having it with me could keep the peace. It was my mentor's weapon of choice with His showdown in the desert. Unfortunately, reading wasn't my strong suit. Fortunately, it was for my bride. This is one of those times that just like the Word of God talks about...she was my helpmate. She loved to read the Word of God and read it to me often. In those early days, it often felt like she was aiming for me. There was always a Scripture to correct my rough edges. I decided that to defend myself and be able to fire back, I had better get to reading. We spent a good deal of wasted time firing rounds on each other before we learned to buddy up and cover each other as we advanced into enemy territory. (Bonus lesson: Shoot your partner enough times and you will find yourself on your own.)

The Good, The Bad and The Ugly (originally *Il Buono, Il Brutto, Il Cattivo*) is Sergio Leone's third and final Spaghetti Western with Clint Eastwood. The movie follows three men: Clint Eastwood, aka as Blondie, is The Good; Lee Van Cleef, aka The Bad; and Eli Wallach, aka The Ugly, are in pursuit of $200,000 of Confederate money and ultimately a shootout.

The Good and The Ugly form an unusual partnership. Clint (Blondie) turns in Ugly (Tuco) and collects the reward money. Just when Ugly is about to be hanged for his crimes, Clint shoots the rope so he can escape and the bounty is distributed equally. But eventually, Blondie and Tuco are at odds with each other.

On the other hand, The Bad (Angel Eyes) is a mercenary who is also in the race for the money which has been hidden in a grave in an unknown cemetery. When The Good and The Ugly are captured by the Union soldiers, The Bad recognizes The Ugly and forces the name of the cemetery out of him by using torture. Since Blondie (the only one who knows the name on the gravestone where the treasure is hidden) wouldn't speak, a three-way shootout is planned for the next day. In Blondie's own words, "$200,000 is a lot of money. We are gonna have to earn it."

Before the guns are drawn, Blondie (Clint Eastwood) writes the key to the treasure, the "name on the grave" on a stone. The last man standing can pick up the stone for the key to finding the loot.

Director Sergio Leone focuses on the guns with hands moving slowly and then to the eyes of the three guys. Blondie doesn't hesitate as he aims and shoots the only real threat, Angel Eyes. (Blondie had already emptied Tuco's gun the previous night and knew he was harmless.) The duel is full of tension and intensity. The battle makes you hold your breath to see the outcome until you realized it was fixed all along in Blondie's favor.

What kind of bravery would I have if I knew the outcome was fixed in my favor? What kind of risks could I take if I knew that failure wasn't fatal? Time for me to "cowboy up."

I had come to a place where I was thankful for the saving grace of Jesus Christ, but it awakened an attitude in me that demanded more out of life – right NOW! Why wait for tomorrow? I could die tomorrow. Live for today! I was no longer willing to play it safe.

It was that thought that lingered in my head, as I sat holding the classified ads section of the Sunday newspaper. I stared at three words spelled out in bold capital letters - CHRISTIAN CONTRACTOR NEEDED. In a moment, I knew these three words could change my life IF I was willing to take the risk.

At that time in my life, my bride and I were newly married, having fun and still learning how to do life together. I was fortunate to be a business owner at 25 years of age and the head of my own construction business. That ownership came with a lot of privileges we enjoyed like nice houses and fast cars. Our inexperience came in the challenges we had not yet learned to handle. A big hurdle was the economic downturn in

Phoenix in the late 1980's. The demand for new builds was down significantly and the inventory of vacant apartments and office buildings was high. I had made good money but lapses between jobs were getting longer each time around. As a result, we struggled because there was just not much money to be made in the industry at the time. In fact, to put it simply, we were starving.

We did the best we could with the money we had and looked for ways to keep our heads above water. We continued to pay for essentials like our cars so we could get to work, but that meant we had to cut down in many other areas. I was getting calls every day from sub-contractors looking for work to feed their families. I couldn't help them either. My wife and I ate at our parents houses a lot because our own refrigerator was bare. Clearly the writing was on the wall for the Phoenix job market. With a young man's bravado, I had a strong will to provide for my wife. I was willing to do anything, no matter the risk or consequence, to turn things around for us. We got on our knees and prayed for a solution.

CHRISTIAN CONTRACTOR NEEDED.

That Sunday morning, I wasn't looking for nor expecting anything other than doing my usual reading of the classifieds – this was a habit I'd learned from my dad. I went back to the ad that had gotten my attention and I kept reading, "Small Christian construction company seeking project foreman; must be willing to relocate to Hawaii."

(Long pause) REALLY? So I ask you, sounded like a pretty perfect job for me, right? Well folks, I have to confess I didn't think so; I had my doubts – seriously. I imagine all of you are on the same side as my beautiful wife, who for two weeks persisted in reminding me to pick up the phone and call them. A possibility is a hint from God, but I just couldn't see it as the right answer. I wasn't ready to pull the trigger.

As things got steadily worse in Phoenix, our struggles became harder. The day came when we decided to stop making payments on our pool. (Hey, we figured the bank couldn't come repossess it!) My bride insistently reminded me again; "Call on the Hawaii job." This time I had to agree, it was finally the right time.

The Lord brought me to a Scripture in Deuteronomy 6: "These are the commands, decrees and laws the LORD your God directed me to teach you to observe in the land that you are crossing the Jordan to possess, so that you, your children and their children after them may fear the LORD your God as long as you live by keeping all His decrees and commands that I give you, and so that you may enjoy long life. Hear and be careful to obey so that it may go well with you and that you may increase greatly in a land flowing with milk and honey, just as the LORD, the God of your ancestors, promised you. Hear, O Israel: The LORD our God, the LORD is one. Love the LORD your God with all your heart and with all your soul and with all your strength. These commandments that I give you today are to be on your hearts. Impress them on your children. Talk about them when you sit at home and when you walk along the road, when you lie down and when you get up. Tie them as symbols on your hands and bind them on your foreheads. Write them on the door frames of your houses and on your gates. When the LORD your God brings you into the land He swore to your fathers, to Abraham, Isaac and Jacob, to give you - a land with large, flourishing cities you did not build, houses filled with all kinds of good things you did not provide, wells you did not dig, and vineyards and olive groves you did not plant - then when you eat and are satisfied, be careful that you do not forget the LORD. Do what is right and good in the LORD's sight, so that it may go well with you and you may go in and take over the good land the LORD promised."

Maybe Hawaii was going to be our PROMISED Land.

The company owner, Mr. Mao, and I spoke on the phone for about 30 minutes. The guy seemed genuine and what he said sounded really good. My wife sat nearby listening, hanging on to every word, silently evaluating my half of the conversation. She was encouraged and I had to admit; it was more than I expected. Before I hung up, Mr. Mao and I made plans to talk again. We talked several more times over the next few days and things progressed. It started to look like this could really happen.

I can remember the guy on the other end of the phone telling me, "We work really hard here (in Hawaii), like 50 hours a week." Wow! That would seem like vacation. I was used to working 75+ hours a week already. By the end of the second week, I was offered the job.

As I sat in my home office in Phoenix, I heard myself accept the job in Hawaii. I gave him my word I would be there in thirty days. "Okay Lord, I am standing on your Word. Here we go."

I hung up the phone and turned to face my beloved wife, who sat perched at the corner of my desk. "Are you okay with this?" I said. "I mean, I didn't ask you before I accepted it – will you go with me?"

Without hesitation, she replied with words that I will remember all the days of my life. She said, "I will follow you where ever you go. My home is not in a place, my home is with you." She reached out to grasp my hand. We turned to face the future, together, in unity. It was a dream come true.

Mr. Mao gambled on us and wanted to move us to Honolulu, lock, stock and barrel – sight unseen. Risky? We had no idea what we had gotten into with this decision, but I had pulled the trigger and counted that the odds were in my favor.

You might be thinking, "Let the party begin!" Right? I mean, think of the endless possibilities with a move to the Hawaiian Islands? Maybe you are more risk averse and you are thinking, "What?? That is crazy. Who would do that? You are in for some big life lessons, kids."

Honestly, we didn't know if we were supposed to go to Hawaii. I mean it wasn't really challenging to have the 'idea' of moving there; after all Hawaii is Hawaii. It was more like, "Why wouldn't I do that?"

The challenge – certainly, it seemed good, but was it BEST to leave Phoenix to move there? Was it worth losing our youth leader positions with the local church to move there? Was it worth losing the closeness with my mom and dad? Was it worth it to take my loving wife away from all her siblings and parents? Could we give up the custom house we had built?

The maverick in me thought, "Heck yes!" I could make some real money and set my future up strong. But I wasn't born to chase money. I was born again to chase God. Hawaii was a long way away – 2,910 miles to be exact. The God in front of me was the real deal. Something big was about to happen in our lives. The Christian thinking that kept me close to my family told me to seek the wisdom of my father. The Word of God clearly advises seeking wise counsel. As the only son, of an only son of an only son, I had a special bond with my dad. I felt certain there was no way my parents were going to be okay with this. I decided to submit my decision not only to my heavenly Father, but my earthly father as well. I had no doubt he loved me and I was precious to him. I walked into their house with a preconceived notion of how this discussion would turn out.

Surprisingly, both my parents highly encouraged us to make the move. Dad put it simply, "Son, if you don't go to Hawaii there will come a day when you'll wonder what it would have been like if you had gone." With his arm around mom, he looked at me and said, "I think you should go." He put his hand on my shoulder and I felt his strength come over me.

I realized it's not up to me, it's up to God. I need not be foolish, I needed to be wise – but above all I needed to be a risk-taker. If I don't take the risk, I'll never see the reward beyond what I can see. Faith needed some action to work with as I stood on the Word of God. I was never going to be left or forsaken. That was the kick in the pants I needed. My wife and I trusted God with our future. With God, who needs a safety net, right?

Leaving the church was another matter. We went to our pastor and told him we were thinking about leaving, but felt conflicted. It was important to us to have him bless us out. On one hand, it was our heart's desire to stay in the safe zone. The church and our work as youth pastors was important to us and we wanted to continue it.

On the other hand we still wanted to be directed by God to know if we were supposed to stay or go. Our pastor had tried for many months to put me on paid staff as the Youth Pastor. I had always refused a salary and did the work anyway. So it was no surprise that he wanted us to stay in Phoenix to work side by side with him. Mistakenly, he thought that our leaving was economic and offered again to put us on paid staff so we wouldn't get into a financial pinch. He said he would to talk to the Elders right away and he was sure they would say yes. As good as it felt to hear that, we felt the need to be upfront and make sure he understood where we were coming from. We explained we were not looking for a job; we were seeking God's hand in our decision making process. We were looking for a sign, an answer on what we were supposed to do.

My wife and I decided that if the Elders said, "No," we would take it as a sign that we were supposed to go, to start a faith journey and move. If the Elders said, "Yes," we would remain. Pastor listened to this plan, prayed with us and agreed that God's will was primary, but he was giddy because he was so sure the elders were going to say, "Yes!"

We believed that only God could make them say no. The day after, we met with Pastor and immediately noticed he looked ragged and upset. He explained, "Through a course that I could never have ever anticipated, the Elders voted to fund a worship director position. They passed on a paid youth pastor." He was clearly stunned and still trying to regain himself from the unexpected answer. At the same time, he knew the position we were holding. We were going to Hawaii. Our faith journey was to begin.

As the days counted down to our departure, the reality of leaving took a toll on my wife. She was already homesick about leaving our house in Arizona . She had spent a great deal of time designing our current house and I had spent a great deal of money constructing it. She was unsettled about leaving her perfect little nest to fly off to parts unknown.

One evening, my parents came over and my dad had a conversation with her. He asked her what she loved most about her house. She looked around the room as she listed all the things she loved about the house, indoors and out. Even though she was smiling, there was a touch of melancholy in her voice. My dad followed her gaze and agreed all the things she mentioned were indeed wonderful. "What a shame you could never do all this again," my dad said.

Confused, my bride responded, "Yes, of course we could. We were the ones who did all this to this house. We certainly could do this again."

Dad said, "So what you're saying about your house is you love everything that YOU did to it?" She nodded her head yes. He clapped his hands together once loudly as he stood up and said, "No problem then, if everything you love is what you did, that's still IN you and you can do that again anywhere!"

Just like that, he gave us the attitude that we were really not leaving anything behind, it was a part of us and we were taking it with us. It wasn't so scary for her then. That was the final answer to a lot of unanswered questions and we were now fully ready to go.

Literally from the time I saw the ad in the newspaper, it was six weeks later that we were having our going-away party. Our families were thrilled about the move; I mean who doesn't want to know someone living in Hawaii? We were excited about the future and what God had in store for us. The Lord was teaching us to trust in Him with all our hearts and not to lean on what we could understand. If we would acknowledge God all along the way, He would direct our path.

At the airport, we were standing at the gangway, when I turned to my lovely bride and asked her to take my hand and let me lead her. She knew what I meant – she knew I was asking her to trust me with our lives and our future. Her answer was clear. She grabbed by hand and held on tight as we boarded the airplane. It was all very symbolic of walking forward, towards a new home and new adventure waiting for us. It felt just like a fairy tale.

What felt like a risk became an adventure when we took the Word of God with us. He was directing our path as we put all our trust in Him. What if there was no risk in the world – what would that look like? Without risk would we recognize the reward? Our beloved Father wants nothing more than to see His children learn and grow, even if there is risk in the process. I mean, let's face it; life can have its scary moments. You can get caught up in circumstances that grab you and take you places you never intended to go, just like being off a bridge and over your head. God's Word was the solid ground under our feet.

Looking back to what could have been or what might have happened is being paralyzed. It was my dad's bold advice to 'go for it' that helped be understand that a step in the Father's direction was all that was needed. There is no safety net when you're on God's path. He guides us so we won't be afraid to walk near the edge. Jim Whittaker, in his autobiography, 'A Life on the Edge: Memoirs of Everest and Beyond' said, "If you aren't living on the edge, you are taking up too much space." I agree.

In the end, God wants us to be confident and capable in everything we do. The Bible is his six shooter against fear. It is also our security in times of trouble. This enforcing weapon represents the Word of God, the Bible. "For the Word of God is alive and active. Sharper than any double-edged sword, it penetrates even to dividing soul and spirit, joints and marrow; it judges the thoughts and attitudes of the heart." (Hebrews 4:12, NIV)

Cowboys carried guns to insure security, not to stir up trouble. Teddy Blue Abbott, a cowboy himself, understood very well the cowboy's motives for carrying firearms. He wrote: "Six-shooters were a great thing for keeping the peace. You wouldn't have any of this calling names and brawling and fighting, where every man was wearing a deadly weapon in plain sight. In the early days men were soft spoken and respectful to each other, because it didn't pay to be anything else." Guns were a defensive measure to ward off potential trouble.

If you were Clint Eastwood, you always had a "friend" to help enforce your words. Especially if you were playing Dirty Harry.

Play Misty for Me opens with a scene where Dirty Harry corners a criminal after a chase and shoot out. He trains his enforcer on the man and says:

"I know what you're thinking. Did he fire six shots or only five? Well, I'll tell you the truth. In all this excitement, I've kind of lost track myself, but being as this is a .44 magnum - the most powerful handgun in the world and would blow your head clean off - you've got to ask yourself one question, 'Do I feel lucky?' Well, do ya punk?"

In ***Sudden Impact***, Harry Callahan has this exchange with a thug:

Dirty Harry: "You boys put those guns down."

Thug: "Say what?"

Dirty Harry: "We're not gonna just let you walk outta here."

Thug: "Who is 'we' sucker?"

Dirty Harry: "Smith, Wesson and me."

Harry pulls a revolver from his inside jacket pocket and begins shooting. He takes out two of the three and corners the third.

Dirty Harry: "Go ahead. Make my day."

The world wants to distract us into forgetting how much ammunition the Word of God has for us or the protection it provides for our soul. We get loose and lay down our pistols, which literally causes all hell to break loose! Worse yet, we get caught up in the world and wander off into the distance away from the battle. Here is an analogy using a bridge...

Date with Death

I get word pictures from God. Pictures are God's way of communicating His timeless truths to me in a way that I best understand.

The first sense I had was the feeling of the warmth against my face – it felt like a welcoming and loving embrace. I opened my eyes to see a beautiful, glorious light as big as the sun. Its brilliance should've blinded me, but it didn't. I could hear music playing softly; although there was no sound. The light bathed my skin as it beckoned me, although no words were spoken. I wanted to go to it; I was ready to walk into its embrace. But between us was a bridge. Without thinking about it, I began to traverse the bridge towards the light. I was drawn to it like a moth.

Peacefully, I walked across a suspension bridge, much like the Golden Gate Bridge. As I walked along, I noticed I was over miry clay rather than water. The ground appeared to be no more than a couple of feet below the bridge. Time had no effect on me as I walked confidently and boldly in my boots towards the other side, knowing that my reward was waiting in the light.

Suddenly something off to the side of the bridge caught my eye. I raised my pistol as I stopped to look. I could see clearly visible, a $20 bill lying on the ground just a few feet from the bridge . I thought, "I'm feeling good, but how much better would I feel with $20?" The bridge was so low, that I could really just step off and grab it – it would only take a second and I would be back on my way towards the light. I decided to go for it.

When I stepped off the bridge, I found the ground was actually soft and squishy. "No problem," I thought, "It's hardly deep enough to slow me down. I'll just lay my six gun here on the edge so I have my hands free and step out just a few feet. It will take only a second."

I stepped out and when I reached down to grab the bill, I saw another object just a few more feet away – it was another twenty. I took one more step away, sunk a bit more and reached down to grab it. Again. as soon as I did, I saw a couple more bills just another arm's length further. Warily, I looked back to the bridge; it was still near and within a short distance, so I continued out a few feet further to grasp some more. Although my boots were now covered in muck, I could still shuffle to the next treasure. To my delight, as I bent down to grab yet another object, something else even bigger and better always appeared in my line of sight. Although I was being enticed by things that were close by, easy to reach and made me sink deeper in the squishy clay, I willingly stepped farther from the safety of the bridge and my weapon to get more.

Soon I was waist deep in the mud with each step harder than the next. I decided to turn back to the bridge. But even with my good intentions, I was immediately captivated by another treasure just a bit farther away. So there was another trinket in my hand, but now I was really stuck. I turned to look back. "God help me!" The bridge was so far away now and I was up to my neck in the mud. "What do I do? Lord, help me. I am going under.....wait...where's my pistol?"

With my focus on the distractions, I had lost sight of the bridge and more importantly...the way to the light.

While Hollywood would have you believe a cowboy carried a handgun for riding the hostile Mexican border, passing through Indian territory or just traveling alone in the wild, he would also have used his rifle or revolver to scare off coyotes, bears, timber-wolves and mountain lions preying on his herd. Frequently, cowboys shot injured stock too weak to finish the trip. The gun was certainly an offensive weapon as well as a defensive one and there was a time I had to use it for protection.

It was at a business lunch at Denny's by the Honolulu Airport when I first met the man I call "the Kiapolo." Mack and I were talking about the upcoming construction projects and this scruffy, unkept, homeless man was seated across the restaurant from us. Downtown establishments generally treated the homeless population with respect, getting them coffee and seating them unless they became belligerent or a nuisance. The Kiapolo seemed harmless enough...then he began making frequent furtive eye contact with me. I began to feel a bit uncomfortable and avoided looking in his direction. "Da kiapolo is making crazy eyes at me!" I whispered to Mack. (Kiapolo is Hawaiian for a person with demonic energy.)

No longer able to have my attention, Kiapolo began to ramble aloud to himself. The waitress came to refill his coffee and calm him a bit but it just set him off. He stood up and began to get louder. Banging the table and speaking gibberish phrases about the government, persecution, and lawlessness, he began to make his way towards Mack and I. It was impossible to ignore him as he gave me a challenging stare down. Mack and I were finished anyway so we decided to make our exit as the Kiapolo starting making a scene.

"How weird was that?" I asked Mack as we drove back to the office. Homeless people don't usually make me fear for my safety but there was something not right with that guy. Later that night I told my bride about the Kiapolo. In her usual way, she had compassion and asked that we pray for him. I agreed, knowing that I would probably never come across him again. The airport area was a good 30-40 minutes away by car and this guy definitely didn't have any wheels.

The next morning I headed towards Kaimana Beach for my morning swim out to the windsock and back. I went early in the morning because it was embarrassing. I used my walking stick to go from the parking lot across the grass to the sandy beach. The beach was another story. Since my legs weren't working so well, traveling across sand was dangerous for me. The only way to the water was across the sand. At the seawall, I would sit and take off my leg brace, tuck my keys and phone in my Bible and lay my walking stick on top of them. Then the humiliating part...I would have to crawl to the water on my hands and knees. Not only was it laborious, it roughed up my knees like sandpaper. Didn't matter though, I was a maverick and I was going in for a swim come hell or high water. (Little did I know that on that day, it would be hell.)

As I emerged from my swim and began my slow crawl back across the sand to the seawall, I could see someone sitting on the park bench. As I crawled closer, I was stunned to see Kiapolo. He was already rocking and ranting out loud but when he noticed that I had noticed him, the pitch intensified. A pit of fear crept into my belly and I had to get my head on straight. I was alone. I was vulnerable. I was weak. What in the world would I do? I did the only thing I knew how. I called on my God my defender. He reminded me of Jesus in the wilderness with Satan. Jesus was calm and chose not to answer any challenge except with God's Word. My Bible was right there on the seawall but it was out of reach. I had to rely on what Scripture was parked in my heart. I began to speak to my own self.

"I will praise the Lord. I have set the Lord before me. He is at my right hand. I will not be moved. My body will rest secure because you will not abandon me. You prepare a table in the presence of my enemies. If you, Lord, are for me then who can be against me. With God on my side, I will not be afraid..." My mind was a jumble of every Scripture I had ever hidden in my heart.

I reached the wall. Kiapolo had not moved from the bench but definitely was fixated on me. It was as if some invisible force had him fenced. I picked up my cell phone and immediately called my prayer warrior friend, Michael Valentino, who was living in Maui. "Pray now, pray loud. I am in danger." Without hesitation, Michael vaulted himself into fervent prayer. I put him on speaker phone while I shoved my useless leg into socks, shoes and a leg brace. I was racing to finish and try to get to my car before Kiapolo came unglued. The beach park was still completely empty in the early dawn light. Michael's prayer calmed me and gave me strength. When I rose to my feet, Kiapolo was unchained. I gathered my things and began to hobble to my car as he closed in on me.

Then a curious thing happened. He became VERY focused and clear speaking. He leaned in as close as he could without touching me. In a hissing and menacing voice he breathed, "How do you like that thing?" He pointed to my leg brace. "My master gave it to you."

I answered him, "Jesus said in Matthew 28:18 that ALL authority in heaven and earth has been given to Him and Him alone."

He was trailing me now as I limped across the asphalt.

ROB and ROBIN MOORE

"His affliction is against you Man of God."

I answered, "That is why for Christ's sake, I delight in weaknesses, in insults, in hardships, in persecutions, in difficulties. For when I am weak, then I am strong."

I opened my car door, threw my phone on the passenger seat with my Bible and plopped down in the driver's seat. As I placed my walking stick inside, I pulled the car door shut while Kiapolo was shouting obscenities. Foul language colored the air and mercifully, my Mercedes door clicked shut and all was silenced but the sound of Michael praying in a holy foreign tongue over me and the situation. Shaking, I started up and threw it into Drive. Resisting the urge to bash Kiapolo with my car, I pulled the phone to my ear to talk with Michael. Wow. What a surreal moment.

I woke my wife up with my wild tale. Kiapolo at the beach park in the early dawn had me at high alert. I knew I had a target on my back. My world had been rocked and more than ever, I knew that my total reliance was on God and God alone. She cried in fear. Fear for me, for our kids, for everything. I was able to assure her that "When FEAR knocks on the door and FAITH answers...there is nobody there." Hope rose up in me that I really was invincible with God on my side. That when I was caught in a duel, my six-guns of the Word were my weapon. The ammunition was limitless. I needed to pack the Scriptures in my gun belt and more than that, I was a crack shot.

I hope that I will always stand strong. I want you to know there is a reason for the hope that rises up in me and it is attached to one person and one person only. The person of Jesus Christ.

I will always praise Jesus with every breath I take. I feel as though the Lord has told me that this is temporal, that He was

174

using it to accomplish His will in my life. "Lord, my prayer is that you would give me some insight to my future, that you might give me a timeline of it, that you would gird me with patience and give to me a greater understanding." He answers me with, "I have promised never to leave you or forsake you." He always answers me with that straight shooting bullet of Biblical truth from His Word. **Wield your weapon. The bullet that takes out the enemy is the voice of the Maverick Mentor in the written Word of God.** That is **lesson number seven**.

Round Up Questions:

1.) What kind of guns do you own?

2.) Have you ever used the Word of God as a weapon? What happened?

3.) Are you good at learning by observation of other's mistakes? What is the biggest risk you have ever taken? How did it turn out?

4.) When fear propels you, how can the Word of God be used to back you up like Smith & Wesson?

5.) What enemy whispers need to be shot down right now in your life?

CHAPTER 9

"The Duel at High Noon"

The Miracles Triumph Over Evil

To a cowboy, a man is not a man unless he can coolly face death and fight for his good name. Fortunately, only a few such shoot-outs ever occurred. Meeting on a street at high noon for a classic gunfight, complete with rules of conduct and emphasis on honor above all else was largely an invention of novelists and journalists and movie directors. Most real duels occur within the human soul.

In one of my favorite Clint Eastwood westerns, **Pale Rider**, calm music plays while a little girl buries her dead dog in the woods. Childlike, she prays: *The Lord is my shepherd, I shall not want.* "But I **do** want." *He leadeth me beside still waters. He restoreth my soul.* "But they killed my dog." *Yea, though I walk through the valley of the shadow of death, I shall fear no evil.* "But I **am** afraid." *Thou art with me. Thy rod and* *thy staff, they comfort me.* "We need a miracle." *Thy loving kindness and mercy shall follow me all the days of my life.* "If you exist." *And I shall dwell in the house of the Lord forever.* "But I'd like to get more of this life first. If you don't help us, were all gonna die. Please. Just one miracle. Amen." As she prays the last few lines, an image of a man (Clint Eastwood) riding a white horse is superimposed on the screen, along with foreboding music. The man on the white horse continues riding through the snow-covered ground into the woods. The unnamed Preacher Man is there to impose justice.

Every human being on earth struggles at one time or another. Like that little girl, they long for a miracle. It can be just as agonizing for adults as they desperately seek justice from an outside source.

Although it may seem like there is a real life adversary to overcome when we face off against another person, like our spouse or a co-worker, many times the battle is completely spiritual. Sometimes I feel like life is like a series of shootouts or spiritual street fights, one after another. The Bible talks of WHEN the battle comes, not IF. There is a clear plan to ward off this street fight. Here is the expanded manual from God's word:

"For though we live in the world / human / flesh, we do not wage war as the world / human / flesh does. Weapons we fight with are not the weapons of the world / human / flesh. On the contrary, they have divine power to demolish strongholds. We demolish arguments / imaginations / human reasoning and every pretension / lofty opinion / high things / vain imaginations that sets itself up / exalts itself against the knowledge of God / rebellious / prideful and we take captive every thought to make it obedient to Christ." 2 Corinthians 13:4

Don't be deceived. There is a real adversary against you. His chief aim is to steal your future, kill the plans God has for you and destroy your life. He uses everything at his disposal in the world, including people, to accomplish his goals.

So how am I going to fight this battle? As a man, I want to confront the enemy head on. "Let's take it outside, big boy."

Imagine high noon outside a saloon on a dirt street. I have been called to a duel to the death with the bad guy. Townspeople line the street, the undertaker is conveniently waiting nearby and my best horse is tied to the post outside the sheriff's office. Got my hat, my jacket, my boots, my gun belt and my six shooters. As I round the corner to face my adversary, my hands are tingling. I know I am a good shot, but is he better? This is where the rubber meets the road.

My Maverick Mentor taught me to "pray in the Spirit on all occasions with all kinds of prayers and requests. With this in mind, be alert and always keep on praying for all the Lord's people." (Ephesians 6:18, NIV) If I am in a battle, I bow my head in prayer. As I walk down the street, God reminds of some Good News.

Good news: "You are not from this place and your Creator has overcome this adversary. What the townspeople (and your evil opponent) don't see is that there is a Preacher Man, a sharp shooter, a marksman, atop the bank building with a rifle and scope on the bad guy. He will bring about my justice for He is my Son."

I breathe a sigh of relief knowing that even if I don't get my gun out of its holster...the battle has already been won. The battle was never mine. My Maverick Mentor has assured my victory, but I still need to walk the road for the townspeople to see this glorious duel be finished.

Incredibly, I was present for one such epic duel after Hurricane Katrina. It was for the very souls of a precious family of four. Let me tell you how the gunfight went.

Imagine a world without sound. There is a stillness that captures your attention and your brain tries to figure out what's wrong, what's missing. It's like void has sound. Your ears try to help your eyes make sense of what you are seeing. Total devastation.

Hurricane Katrina

After the hurricane, the Gulf region needed two things – clergy and a builder. I was both. It was a no-brainer. I was drawn to go.

I decided to take one of my foreman with me to scout out the situation. While sitting on the plane, I was thinking how powerful it would be to bring thirty journeymen carpenters with me and stay a week. So much could be accomplished in that time. My guys would equal the workforce and strength of 10x untrained volunteers.

Then, I arrived and saw the devastation. What an eye-opener! In all my years on this earth, I've never seen such...emptiness. It's not just absence of life. It's just absence. The pictures from the news doesn't quite prepare you for the moment when you see it for real. Everything was gone or in complete shambles. Looking up and down the streets – gone were the sounds of life: no children playing, no dogs barking, no people. There were some crazy sights: houses completely upside down, cars in trees and miles of sidewalks to nothing. The hurricane didn't just wash life away; it sucked it completely out of the area. Places no longer looked like neighborhoods; they looked like the aftermaths of a war zones. Wind, rain and floodwater left homes irreparably damaged. By day, people came and worked on their houses. By night, the sense of desertion was overpowering. Even a graveyard would feel less desolate, because it is not meant for the living.

Normally, I don't have any problem keeping my emotions in check. This time, I could not help it. I wept.

One couldn't put a Band-Aid on this; there was 20 years of work re-building here at best. Initially, I thought I was going to be cool and send 30 guys out for a week, then I realized that was like spitting in the ocean.

Help Was On The Way

It was exhilarating to see armies of volunteer groups charging out every morning from our volunteer headquarters, assigned to a specific location to work for the day. Many of the streets were now unidentifiable, no names. It was hard for even the locals to say where you were and where you were going because almost every existing landmark had been demolished in the storm. In our confusion with directions and streets, we came upon our jobsite for the day. As we approached the house, the family was waiting outside in the front yard. They seemed unsure whether to greet us or not but we unloaded. Hey, there was work to be done and we were armed and ready.

The young father stood tall and gave each of us a firm handshake, while his young wife and two small children stood by. Honestly, they seemed dazed and overwhelmed. Their expressions changed when we said four little words, "We're here to help."

You see, William Jackson Landry was a third generation Louisianan, born to a family with a long history in Chalmette. Will's Papaw Jack built the little yellow house near Paris Road in St. Bernard Parish. With eyes brimming, he turned toward the house and began to tell us about this sad little structure we saw before us.

"The house was small, but somehow was always big enough to hold the whole family when gathering for Sunday dinners. Granny would say there was always room for one more." That was the theme of this blue-collar community who held potluck dinners to benefit families in need and where local fishermen and shrimpers give part of their daily catch to the less fortunate. Neighbors could trace their roots back to their great-grandparents and beyond. It was not uncommon for generations of families to live on the same street. Will had many memories of growing up in this house. In one way or another, this house was where his life milestones happened – he had a deep connection to it, it was a part of him. As a child, Will would prefer to nap on the floor, laying his belly against the cool linoleum in the summer time. He even brought Sissy LeShay here to meet his grandparents. The ribbing he got from his cousins for having a girlfriend when he was only 10 years old – that seemed like it was just yesterday. These memories tugged at his heart as he tried to keep the tears in.

It was said if you return to find your house standing, you were one of the lucky ones. Lucky? Will didn't look like he felt very lucky. Standing in front of his house, it was not recognizable to him. How proud he was to have restored to the original yellow color his Mama loved and his Papa Jack had so loyally maintained. What hurt the most was the large red "X" painted on the front of the house – his mamaw's house. In St. Bernard Parish, the houses were painted bright to reflect the spirit of South Louisiana – today it's bearing the spray paint markings from the search and rescue teams.

It was an assault to every one of his living senses. The front porch was gone, only the roof over it remained, sagging and broken; the holes were so large you could see clear through to the blue sky behind it. The proud and brilliant yellow appeared colorless beneath the dried mud.

On the inside, everything was trashed and completely useless. Everywhere piles of debris. Remnants of things that no longer fit together or that no longer made sense. Just broken pieces that now symbolized a life that was also fragmented and gone. Nothing fit anymore in his life – or made sense. Now, his parents were gone and this was his house – his home, where he and Sissy lived with their two kids; Little Jack, age 8, and Sadie, age 5. His little yellow house was destroyed and with it, all hope of a bright future. What was he do? He broke down.

We're Here to Help

Nothing happens by accident when we're in the hands of God. On one hand, I had never seen a couple as beaten down and full of hurt as Will and Sissy. On the other hand, our team of volunteers had arrived at the Landry's to do the gut-out with immeasurable cheer and goodwill. They had with them the resources, manpower and building materials to do the job. First item on the agenda was to start the work with a prayer of thanks. Then, the team hit it hard. They began to rip out the belly of the house and throw out anything and everything; including carpet, sheet rock, cabinets, etc. The team worked joyfully with precision and harmony. At first, the family stood shell-shocked watching their beloved place get gutted to the bones. It wasn't long before camaraderie grew between the team members and began to infect the Landry's. The team encouraged the family to join in. Gently at first, then with a vengeance they joined in this cathartic exercise to move them forward out of their pitiful state. Even the children got into the spirit and willingly relinquished their damaged play things by adding them to the piles on the street. The crew and the Landry's worked all day, side by side. At the end of the day, the house was clear and ready for the restore and re-building phase. Praise God, it felt good!

Before they left, the entire group gathered in prayer. It was then that Will and Sissy painfully shared with embarrassment that they thought the team must have come to the wrong house. They claimed that they certainly had never expected or asked for help from the volunteer center. They couldn't imagine how the team ended up on their block. After calling back to headquarters for clarification, it appeared the team had been scheduled at another location after all. The air was filled with the laughter of goodwill as the team acknowledged that tomorrow was another day and they would to the other house eventually. All agreed that God knew what He was doing and they were glad to have been sent by Him to the Landry Family. The goodwill continued as the team invited the family to the church service that evening. The Landry's looked at each other hesitantly, then accepted.

Testimony

At service that night at volunteer headquarters, there was praise and worship and an outpouring of God's Spirit from the many believers of many denominations who wanted to praise His name. At a particular time, the microphone was opened up to people who wanted to share what the Lord had been up to that day. Will and Sissy held hands tightly as they waited for their turn. They finally stood and spoke to the assembly. At first, their story was much like countless other residents from St. Bernard Parish who had lost everything in the storm. Will explained how his family lived in the same house his whole life; he married and was now raising his two kids there. After a pause, he gazed at Sissy and then with a quivering voice began to speak, "We had nothing to salvage in our little yellow house... absolutely nothing." His tone was filled with loss and despair. Choking up, he said, "I was so beaten down. I was totally helpless. When the volunteers came to help, the relief was overwhelming. They gave my family hope." Sissy clutched his arm and looked on as he spoke about the team and how they were a God-send.

The couple explained that they were drawn to come to service that night, not because they knew the Lord, but they had seen His good works in the crew and the HOPE they brought into their home. Will paused and said "You see, they did more than help us clear out a house, they actually saved our lives." The couple quietly revealed they had made a suicide pact just a short time before the crew arrived on their street. They had made the agreement they would take the lives of their two children at sundown then they would take their own lives because they had lost all hope. They couldn't bear to wake up to another morning. Nobody had come to help. Nothing had been done. The sheer enormity of what was before them to start over again took every bit of breath out of them and was terrifying. They were lost and afraid and completely devoid of any promise for a future for them and their babies. They didn't know where to turn.

The miracle was that after they had made that very emotional decision, that very day the Lord had sent people to help and to work on their home and to love on them without them even knowing how it happened. It totally transformed them. It changed their future. What could have been a night of pain and tragedy for a young family turned out to be a mighty victory and celebration for the Lord. They were overwhelmed with love and support and knew they would never be so alone again.

To conclude his testimony right before he and his wife prayed to accept the Lord Jesus Christ, Will said, "I want every one of you to know, this isn't just about rebuilding people's homes – it's about restoring a sense of hope to the community that feels hopeless." In a devastated community, once you get one family back into their home, then other families are willing to come back as well. There's a very nice ripple effect.

One little yellow house at a time...with the right people, at the right place at just the RIGHT time. Bravo Father!

In this battle, the adversary came for a family but people turned out and shifted the battle into the Lord's hands. He is always the victor. There was another time when I walked into a battle that had already begun. Actually, I drove.

The Ordinary Miracle

To let you in on a little secret, I have another passion. I love to scuba dive. A number of years ago while on vacation with my wife in the Caribbean, I had the opportunity to scuba dive for the first time. I LOVED it. When I get it in my mind to do something, I am ALL IN. So, I went through all the certifications from Open Water Diver to Advanced Diver to Rescue Diver to Dive Master and finally to Professional Dive Instructor. Today with scuba diving on my mind, I decided to take off work early and head for the dive shop - hey even mavericks in the construction world deserve to get away! Being Arizona, it wasn't unusual that we were in the middle of a terrible heat wave and it was as a real scorcher as I got in my truck to drive across town from Phoenix to Mesa, AZ. Despite the heat, I'm enjoying the drive singing with the radio. As I move along, I see the hard core athletes are not deterred by the melting heat but are out in full force, and why not? It's a beautiful day to be alive – Praise God!

I'm in my truck, taken in by the heat of the day and the lull of the slow moving traffic when I hear the sound of skidding tires and screeching brakes. The car in front of me ran a red light and hit a young woman on a bicycle. I immediately throw my vehicle in park, jumped out of my truck, and ran over to help. I find the young woman sprawled across the pavement.

Lying in the street next to her was a pile of mangled mess of metal, wheels and spokes. From my rescue training in diving, I knew it was bad. She was lying on her side, crying and screaming in pain, drenched in sweat. She is hurt bad and it is critical not to move her. I am trained for emergency situations. I am the first man on the scene. My lightning fast evaluation went something like this: It is 114° in the shade so it has to be at least 300° on that hot black asphalt she is laying on. Before I can evaluate her injuries, I have to do something about her being baked to death on the pavement. Before she could suffer 3rd degree burns, I had already devised a plan. Being in the construction business, I always had my trusty Igloo water cooler in the back of the truck and an ice chest filled and ready to go. I ran to my truck, grabbed my water and ice chest and raced back to where she was laying. I carefully poured the ice and the water all around her body, hoping that it would insulate her from the pavement and cool her body down. It worked. Now we can wait for the ambulance.

As I finished, people were starting to crowd around and I was glad to see the ambulance pull up. Somebody had called 911. The noise the crowd made sounded like bees buzzing as the paramedics made their way to her side. I stood by as they carefully turned her over and I was struck by the pronounced shape of what looked like a very broken pelvis bone protruding out from her hip area. She was obviously in great pain and having difficulty. The concerned crowd turned into gawkers as the paramedics began to assess her injuries. The instinct to protect a vulnerable person overcame me so I started pushing people back to allow her some dignity and privacy. I moved in a circle around her and pushed hard, but the onlookers resisted and shifted around me to get a better look. I didn't know what else to do, so I began to pray out loud that God would show up and heal her. I prayed He would take care of the circumstances in this situation. The paramedics lifted her onto the gurney and made their way to the ambulance and I followed. I stood by as they loaded her into the ambulance and was surprised when the paramedic turned to me and said "She wants to talk to you." She was awake, alert and somewhat calm. I tried not to look at the menacing shape her injury made under the white sheet that covered her. The pain of it had to be unbearable for her. I couldn't think of what to say so the words "I'll get your bike" spilled out. Speaking slowly and with some difficulty, she told me her name was Heather and asked if I would take her bike to her father who was down the street shopping at the local big box warehouse club. She gave me his name and asked me to inform him what happened and tell him what hospital to find her at. The paramedics were ready to go so I loaded her bike up in my truck and headed to find her father.

Once there, I ran into the store and asked if they could page her father. They explained they had no paging system to do that. Are you kidding me? How could a warehouse this large not have a paging system? I'm on a serious mission here! Adrenaline pumping, I am looking for a solution. I grabbed a sheet of paper and carefully wrote his name in large capital letters - HENRY HOCHE. I can't remain static so I took off to look for him, running up and down every aisle in the store, stopping to show the paper to every shopper I came to. I went through the entire store - no response. I thought, what am I to do now? She's depending on me to find her father!

Adrenaline gone and feeling out of options, I went back to the front of the store. What if he's not even here? I stopped next to the front counter, and decided to do what I should have done in the first place. I stood and prayed – "Lord, please help me, what do I do next? How am I going to help her?"

I'm going to pause here a second and describe the scene from the father's point of view. Picture this. You are a dad, spending the afternoon shopping at the big box warehouse. An anxious, over-heated, sweat-drenched 25 year-old stranger with wild eyes is standing near the exit holding a sign with your name on it. Do you approach him? What could he want with you?

I finish my prayer and take a deep breath. Immediately a man walks up to me, points to the paper I was holding and said, "That's me, I'm Henry." The last thing he was expecting was for me to tell him was his daughter was hit by a car and is on the way to the hospital – oh and I have her bike! We immediately left the store and headed for the parking lot – his extreme concern and the emotion of it was clearly on his face. We tried but couldn't get the bicycle in his car, so I agreed to follow him to the hospital and we'd deal with it there so he could get quickly to his daughter. Clearly, the concern for her was priority.

We arrived at the hospital and rushed inside. As her father, Henry was immediately escorted to his daughter's room and I went to the nearby waiting room. I wasn't sure if I should stay or go but something kept me there. After about 30 minutes, I was stunned to see Heather WALK out into the waiting room with her dad at her side. The same girl I had seen injured and lying broken on the asphalt was now standing and walking toward me. I was floored. She gave me a big hug and through smiling tears she thanked me for helping her and for praying for her. She explained that while lying in the street and through the pain, she could hear me praying over her. Tears were running down her face as she spoke and I could see in her eyes the light of glory – she GOT IT – she knew a miracle had happened. I too was in tears because God had allowed me to witness that miracle being performed before my eyes. There was no doubt in my mind that her pelvis had been broken. I was amazed to see that now, her pelvis was fine.

Standing looking at her, there were no burns, only some scrapes and bruises, but otherwise she was about to be released to go home. God had totally healed her! I had not even realized that I had a running conversation going with God during the whole process. Because I am an ALL IN kind of person, I did all I could in my own strength but God is the one who took my humble efforts and zapped them with his DYNAMITE power. I gave God all the glory for His healing presence in Heather's body. The awe of it still brings me to my knees. God doesn't need my assist but He sure loves to show off when we involve ourselves in the process. I had my plans for scuba diving that day but God had a better one. A plan for diving deep in Him. He wanted to show me that miracles are ordinary for Him.

The ordinary miracle – there is such beauty and magnificence in that simple statement. The miraculous for us is every day for Him. Just like the little girl in *Pale Rider* who prayed for a miracle, she will live the rest of her life knowing the impossibility of the incredible grace that she received from Him that day. No one can ever change that. For me, well my faith continues to grow. God has given me the gift to see the bigger miracle...the sharpshooter above me who takes out the bad guys.

We have our plans. Our agendas. Our timelines. Are we willing to be interrupted by our Creator to participate in an eternal duel?

When I found myself in battle, I knew I needed to keep the line of communication open to my boss. Sure, He gives me promptings through His Holy Spirit but we are also told to pray. Satan hates it when we pray. He knows that it strengthens us and keeps us alert to his deception. It is like having those little "ears" in to allow another person with a better vantage point to give you secret information. The Apostle Paul reminds us also to pray for others as well. We can be ready for whatever the enemy shoots at us when we are ready for a gunfight.

As a maverick, I was already wearing my spiritual boots all of the time. They kept me bold. My spiritual fringed leather jacket protected my soft underbelly by reminding me that righteousness (God's way of doing things) is always best. I kept my six-shooter of God's Word close to my gut in my gun belt of truth that I had surrounding my loins. My squint towards the future was alerting me to the fiery attacks of the enemy and my cowboy hat made my transformation complete. Fully suited up, I was ready to stroll down past the saloon of despair.

Any Given Sunday

Most everyone knows that pastors work on any given Sunday, but sometimes when on Sabbatical we are hidden in the flock of another gathering of believers. That's exactly how I thought of myself that Sunday, incognito and hidden in a group. I can hear God chuckle at the thought. I had taken my eldest son to church one Sunday at a local Assembly of God for their exuberant vibrant worship. At the time, it was more for my son than myself. My current congregation was full of small children and adults. My son was turning thirteen and desperately longing to belong to a youth group. We had heard this congregation had a thriving one and we were there to check things out. Or so I thought.

The service began and we were worshiping when I notice the guy to my right was crying his eyes out. Now I am aware that worship can be very emotional and it's not uncommon to see someone crying, but he was sobbing uncontrollably. My gut told me it was more than the music that was driving his emotion. Not only did I feel very much like I should talk to him – I felt like God prompted me to engage him. I whispered to him and placed a consoling hand upon his back. He began pouring out his heart in hushed tones.

I learned his name was Eddie and he had lost his job. That didn't seem so severe but the real blow to add insult to injury was that he had just learned his beloved wife of 8-years had been diagnosed with breast cancer. Shaking, he explained that her doctors said she would need to have a single (possibly a double) mastectomy and she needed to have it immediately. Eddie felt like their lives were falling apart – could all this be really happening?

They had come to church today; desperate to find some peace and some sense of understanding, but he felt overwhelmed. As I comforted him, I began to pray over him. I heard the Lord prompt me to pray for her, the wife. I got the impression that if I do it NOW and anoint her with oil, He will heal her. I asked Eddie where his wife was and he turned and introduced me to Loralei.

So here I am. At a crossroads. I had come with my son, thinking it was all about him. Eddie captured my attention with his emotion and then I thought it was all about him. Then he tells me about the cries of his wife's heart and I feel now it is all about her. Reaching for the vial of anointing oil I keep on my key chain, I begin. I anoint her with oil, hold her hands and I start praying for her. Then it hits me. Here I am trying to make a connection with my son, ministering to Eddie, praying for Loralei...only to learn the real issue is that on any given Sunday, actually any given DAY, it is all about Jesus.

In an instant, He changes my perspective. It is not about

anything but HIM. There is something so beautiful and powerful about being in a moment when you feel His presence.

He changed my perspective in an instant. In my mind's eye I could see from God's view from above. Imagine being way up high looking down into a very large room which is filled to capacity. People are standing with arms raised and moving around at their own will, praising, singing, and dancing. Somewhere in the midst of all this, you zero in on a group of people huddled together in a circle with hands on each other's shoulders and heads bowed. They have bowed their will to the will of God. They are reaching into the throne room and asking for mercy, for grace, for healing. They are unified and aligned and speaking Your Word back to you. They remember a promise about your stripes healing them. About their weakness being Your strength and it inclines Your heart toward them.

I finished praying. I know He is here. He hears. Clearly and almost immediately I hear God say, "She's healed." SHE IS HEALED! It was just that simple; no big TA-DA! – just, "She's healed." That's our Father!

So I stop and looked right at her and said "You're healed – the Holy Spirit just told me. YOU ARE HEALED." She looks back at me with 100% belief in her eyes. With tears streaming down her cheeks, she tries to speak and manages to whisper a "thank you." Eddie stands with a calm radiance over him. We continue to huddle a little longer, this time my focus was totally on Him, thanking Him for my breath, my life, these people, His mercy for us sinners. After worship, there were hugs all around. I turned back to my son and we listened to the rest of the service. I left not knowing what would ever come of it but I knew God would have the glory.

Since my wife loves these God moments as much I

do, I couldn't wait to get home and share with her. My son enthusiastically joined in with the details and I knew God had had a moment with him also. Curiously, he thought he had recognized the mom, Loralei, as another homeschooling mom that my wife casually knew. My wife had no idea that the woman had been going through so much but sent her a card with a kind and encouraging word later that week. What a small world our Lord gives us sometimes. A short time passed and I received this return letter from Loralei:

Dear Pastor Rob,

I don't know if you remember me but last year in August you prayed for me at church. We were visiting and you were sitting in front of us. You didn't know my husband and I, but we knew your wife through homeschool.

I had just been diagnosed with breast cancer in my left breast and the surgeon quickly scheduled me for a mastectomy. I got a second opinion. This surgeon agreed with the first surgeon however, she suggested consulting an oncologist on the possibility of shrinking the lump through chemotherapy then doing surgery to remove the lump. So I decided to take that route. I started chemo. I was to go through 4 rounds of chemo initially. When you met me I had one more round of chemo to go. That morning at church, you had asked my husband Eddie if we needed prayer and he told you I was battling cancer. You anointed me with oil and prayed for my healing. You told my husband and I that I was healed and to "Trust in Jesus." In the months ahead we continued to hold on to those words.

After completing the 4th round of chemo, my lump was smaller but not enough to remove just the lump. The recommendation was still a mastectomy My husband and I continued to hold on to trust in Jesus. We continued to pray and confess God's Word over my body..."by His stripes I've been healed" and many other healing scriptures over and over. I knew I was healed I just didn't know how and when it would manifest in the natural.

Finally, came the breakthrough! After a few months, the lump got smaller and smaller until I couldn't feel it anymore. I went back to my oncologist who scheduled me for a mammogram (this was to help the surgeon) so that I could move forward with surgery. I went in for a mammogram the day after Christmas. After I waited in the room for a long time, the technician came back and apologized for the long wait but she needed the doctor to review my pictures before I left. She told me that my left breast tissue was the same as my right breast tissue! I said Praise God!! She said maybe the chemo did it or maybe it was inflammatory cancer. But we know that God is good and His mercy endures forever!!

I just wanted to share with you my praise report and thank you for taking the time that Sunday morning to pray for me and speaking those words to my husband and I to know that I shall not die but live and declare the works of God. May God bless you and may He continue to pour out His anointing upon you.

Loralei

It's not me not what I did. It's Jesus and who He is. The sharpshooter on the roof took out the target and if I get out of the way and just follow Him, I can be used as a vessel to accomplish His miraculous. Loralei said it well – to know Him is to be set free to live life as He intended. On any given Sunday, on any given day, He is Lord. AMEN

Just when you start to get full of yourself and your

shooting abilities, the Lord reminds you that the battles are not yours. For me, He allowed me to take a spiritual gut punch so hard that I limped to the duel at high noon.

Not For Faint of Heart

Previously, I shared my story of accepting Christ and how my journey began.

Fast forward twenty years. My life is very different now. Gone is the young cowboy, naïve and of the world. What lives and breathes is a raging maverick for God. My walk has matured. I've changed my life and I'm actively on His team. He's my heavenly Dad and He's come through so many times that my "Godfidence" (my confidence in God) is HUGE!

For this story, I'll share with you another time of how that Godfidence was strengthened. Most of my life, I had been an avid runner but I began to have an issue with my legs. It concerned me enough that I went to see a doctor. (More about my legs later). I don't know about you, but for me, going to see a doctor is never a treat. Here I was, in the small, cold exam room and the doctor was asking me question after question. I made what I thought was an off-handed comment about how my hands went numb while I slept. In case you didn't know, when a doctor suddenly makes eye contact with you and frowns, that's not good.

I quickly clarified my comment and said, "It only happens when my hands are folded across my chest; but if I had them down my sides I am okay." With great concern, he sternly advised me to go see a Heart Specialist today. Immediately.

So, off I went to be examined by another doctor, a heart specialist, who happened to be a Harvard graduate. I couldn't do the treadmill stress test because of the stumbling issue with my legs, so he decided to do a nuclear stress test with medication. Just a few hours from the time I walked in to my first appointment for my legs, I found myself laying on a bed having a major test done on my heart. Prone as if dead, but with my heart racing like I was running hard, they put me through the test. After it was all done, Doctor Harvard explained the main artery appeared to be significantly blocked. At minimum, he advised immediate surgery to clean out the pipes and recommended a possible stent insertion to hold open the arteries. I took a slow second to respond and said, "I'll have to pray about this." I'll never forget Doctor Harvard's response. He said, "Are you a fool? You don't have time to pray about this – you could die." Well, I always make time to pray to my Dad. So I left his office and I went home to do just that. Truth be told, I was a little shaken up and I thought to myself, "I'll get a second opinion with another heart doctor."

So two days later, Heart Doctor #2 said, "Are you a fool? This is not invasive, you have to do this – you could die on your way home." Well, he was certainly in my face about it, but I wasn't sold on the idea yet. I went home, prayed again and then decided to get yet another opinion. I made an appointment with a third heart doctor. Do you ever keep asking the same question to different people hoping someone will give you the answer you really want? Well, I was looking for the doctor that was going to say, "NO, you don't need this!"

As you may have guessed, Heart Doctor #3's diagnosis was like all the others, but he added, "Look at me, I'm much younger than you are and I have seven stents in my own chest. I wouldn't be here if I didn't have them." Great. I sat in his office looking at the many diplomas on the wall. Maybe he was right. Since it was early December, I told Doctor Harvard I didn't want to have surgery before Christmas. What if things went wrong? That would be the worst Christmas ever. Then my 20th wedding anniversary was in early January. I wanted to make it to twenty. I told the doctor that late January was the earliest I would consider. Secretly, I also wanted to give time for God to do a miracle. The doctor somberly said, "It is your decision but you are taking your life in your own hands." No, I thought...my life has always been in God's hands.

In the following days, I had a missionary from Israel come into our cafe and want to pray for me. Specifically, he wanted to place his hands on my chest and pray. He had no idea. A pastor friend of mine came off the podium at his ordination and laid his hands on me and prayed for my heart with a room full of believers joining in. It was both humbling and wonderful. My wife and children prayed continually for God to do a radical thing. Their faithful, earnest prayers were always ringing in my ears.

Two days after my wedding anniversary, with my beautiful bride of 20+ years at my side, we arrived at the hospital for the procedure. Doctor Harvard, my surgeon, stopped by while they prepped me. He explained they would give me a little happy juice to ensure I wouldn't feel anything and that I'd be awake for the whole procedure so they could communicate with me. My wife waited with me and we were cutting up and acting light-hearted. As they were about to wheel me in, she kissed me and said "Remember, if you see the bright light, turn away. Promise me! Ha! Ha!" I laughed. It felt good. I praised God for her because only she could say that to me at a time like this and make me laugh.

I was wheeled into the room and Doctor Harvard explained he had scheduled the Operating Room (O.R.) so if we get in there and find it's bad we can go right in to open heart surgery in the O.R. Well, can we just hold on a darn minute please?! Open heart surgery? Feeling desperate and with a great need to defend myself, I said to Doctor Harvard, "You told me your stress test was only correct 90% of the time – I'm banking on the 10% that nothing is wrong." He stepped up to the challenge and said "As your surgeon, I'm banking on the 90%."

They were ready to start. As I was wheeled into place, I laid on my back and looked at the ceiling. Forcing me to turn my head to the side, I could just barely make out the shape of a machine as it descended. My eyes closed and I began to pray. I immediately felt the warmth from a large light close to my face – I thought to myself, "There must be a ray of light coming from the machine." I opened my eyes and the room was very dark, almost black, but I could see a very faint soft halo of light coming from the monitors on the wall across the room. I closed my eyes again and poof! The bright warm light was back again. I got it! I remembered my wife saying, "If you see the bright light, turn away!" I said, "Dad? Is that you?" Then God spoke. He said, "It's Me." I could not speak for a moment for my throat was thick with emotion. I peered into the light (with my eyes closed) and said, "If you're calling me home I'm ready, but I would really like to stay here and raise my kids." That magnificent voice responded, "I'm not calling you home, I just wanted you to know that I am right here." The peace and well-being that came with that statement left me drifting and feeling weightless.

Suddenly the room lights came on, the machine retracted above me, and Doctor Harvard walked up to my side. Wow, that seemed quick. He was still wearing a mask, so I couldn't see his face, but I could see his eyes – wide and wild. He said to me, "Mr. Moore, I can't explain this, nor will I try – but you have ZERO blockages and you can go home after some time in post-op." He went on to excitedly explain that my arteries were not blocked. In fact, they were larger than normal which allowed for more blood flow. But what really perplexed him (he looked at the monitors as if to convince himself again) was that I didn't have the normal number of arteries surrounding my heart. I had grown two more! He discussed the improbability of all this – yet there it was plainly visible on the monitors for anyone to see.

Discussing it later with a doctor friend, we came to the conclusion that there must have been a blockage at one point. The arteries must have grown larger with the increased load they had to bear and the incredible body pump even grew new pathways to help get around the blockage.

But somehow, in God's mysterious way, the blockage had disappeared and left some nice super-sized arteries and a few extra ones. God doesn't just answer prayer; he answers "exceedingly and abundantly more than we can ask or imagine." (Ephesians 3:20)

My job is to believe; I leave it to him to do the impossible. The enemy won't win this showdown.

I'm typing and talking to God at the same time. Again, I asked God for a download on who in the Bible went through battles. I grabbed the Bible and opened it to Genesis. God said "Just start reading the names."

He said, "Do you see? Men of God have to wake up the spiritual dog and feed it the most. Be righteous and do things my way. Reality can't be your truth, my Word must be what you stand on. Even with the struggles, be BOLD! Know who holds your future. Don't just be transformed, but bring the Kingdom of God near to others so they might also be transformed. Use the Word of God as your defender and most of all, remember how the ending goes...I have already won the fight."

Now I got it. When you are on God's team, you GET TO

be mentored by a maverick.

Like it or not, every single one of us is involved in this intense spiritual struggle. The battleground is not earthly real estate; it is the human heart. Winning possession of a heart is a battle that is spiritual. Once our heart is won for Jesus, we are His. For me, I know who I ride for. My loyalty is to my brand. No matter what the price, I will pay it. I am a maverick and proud of it.

"You therefore must endure hardship as a good soldier of Jesus Christ. No one engaged in warfare entangles himself with the affairs of this life, that he may please Him who enlisted him as a soldier" (2 Timothy 2:3, 4, NKJV)

I would tell people, "I am not from this place." More than that, I do not battle like the world does. Even though I have already lived a more vibrant life than most, my best days are yet to come.

My Pastor called me a "drink offering" being poured out unto Jesus. AMEN! I know Jesus will just one day speak it and I will run again. Like my God spoke the world into existence, with the Holy power of the spoken word, it says we will see things greater through Him on this earth with His power and His incredible love for me.

But the battle for me is fierce. It is like a duel at high noon with a larger than life adversary. It is daunting walking down this road alone with the townspeople watching from the shadows to see if I will make it to the afternoon.

Know what? They don't see my sharpshooter on the roof. He is my ace in the hole. I know the showdown is already over and who the winner is, but I still have to walk it out so the townspeople can know.

They have to gasp and heave a sigh of relief when the foe is overtaken in the duel. They have to know that **the battle is not ours but it belongs to the Lord**. That is the **final lesson** of my Maverick Mentor.

Round Up Questions:

1.) Can you recite the Psalm 23? Where and when did you learn it?

2.) Have you ever gotten drawn into someone else's duel? What happened? Why did the Lord choose you to be there?

3.) What gunfights are you in the middle of right now?

4.) Who does the battle really belong to that you are fighting? Have you been using all the weaponry of heaven or depending on the sharpshooter?

5.) If you were free to do anything today, what would you do?

ROB and ROBIN MOORE

CALL TO ACTION

Some days I feel like I am walking around with a squint looking for an imaginary duel at high noon. "Do you feel lucky, punk? Go ahead, make my day." Often I find myself "on the outside looking in" at people who follow a traditional path. Are you like me, looking for someone who understands the risk-taking, slightly rebellious, edgy, wild side of you? Could you also be yearning for a mentor who challenges and inspires you every day?

Maybe you too are a maverick, an original who doesn't do what is expected. Maybe you are that guy that isn't scared to cross the line of conformity. With the maverick running in your veins, you rebel against the herd mentality. Maybe you have resisted "church" or "religion" for this very reason. Let me assure you, our Maverick Mentor understands your needs. He created you! He doesn't want to fence you in to a set of rules, he wants you to be free. Your Maverick Mentor wants to meet you at this moment and show you the truth of who he really is. Will you trust him with your soul?

In this showdown of good and evil, the enemy has slung lies and half-truths to every maverick to keep him wild and rebellious and far away from God. If you knew how much like Jesus you really were, the enemy would have no more hold over your life. Today is your High Noon. Are you ready to align with the one Mentor who understands you better than you do yourself?

It is time to put your enemy on notice that your mouth is about to be speaking truth. Say this declaration of faith aloud with the boldness of a maverick:

JESUS, you are above all. Forgive me for being wise in my own eyes and thinking I didn't need you. I turn away from thinking that my maverick spirit didn't line up with your way of thinking. I now realize you made me this way! I want to accept you as the Lord of my maverick heart . I bow down to you alone. I confess that my pride has kept me from being mentored by you for my best life. Humbly, I ask that you reign and rule over me from this day forward. Give me eyes to see and ears to hear what it is you want from me. I vow to be loyal to you and nothing keep me from following you. Help me to seek your way of doing things for it really is the best way. Let me speak words of truth, not just reality. Place your salvation on my head and transform me as I squint for a future I do not yet see but believe in faith is coming. Let me walk out this gospel and shoot straight with your Word starting now. Amen.

Signed: _____

Date: _____

Final Word from Rob

Seeing His Awesome hand in my life has changed my existence, focused my wants, and transformed my desires. Life has gone from being all about me to truly being all about Him. He has always been so lovingly gentle with me, even through my own misconceptions of who I am. John the Baptist said it so well, "the One whose sandals I am unworthy to untie." (John 1:7)

Although I had thought my bravado, my talent and my sheer determination had got me where I was, I realized that it was worth as much as filthy rags. (Isaiah 64:6)

Today, He is still training me to become the man He wants me to be. I am a student learning to hear Him, doing what He says to do, when He says to do it. The hardest part? Doing it His Way versus my way. Like the room in my vision, I now anticipate the incredible from the impossible. I love it when my impossible collides with HIS POSSIBLE!

God Gave Me Visions

January 1997: The First Vision

I found myself sitting in the center of an incredibly exquisite large round room. I took a rushed glance around. The meticulous raised panel walls were carved of mahogany. The domed ceiling was very high, back lit, and painted with a detailed mural in it's center. The ornate floor was white Thassos marble.

My eyes locked on a set of doors at the far side of the room. I was compelled to rush over to them to see what was on the other side. Ripping open the doors, I jumped backward in fear as I realized that the room was high up in the sky with nothing but air for the first step. There was a city below in the distance but exiting would be a fatal mistake. As the room seemed to pitch me forward out the opening, I quickly worked my way back to the center of the room and sat completely down on the floor. But, like a moth to a flame, I was drawn to the opening two more times. Each time, the dizzying height of nothingness magnified my fear and I would crawl back to the center of the room. I cried out, "Why am I so afraid?"

I heard God respond to me, "This is one of your problems, Son. You are always rushing to do the next thing, never taking the time to enjoy the moment that I have created for you right now. You always want to do things your way and consequently get in My way. It is time to slow down and be filled".

From that moment, I was filled. I was filled with His peace as I started to study the room in detail. Upon closer inspection, the floor was amazing! The transparent marble looked as though it was four feet thick. The intricate detailing of the wall woodwork was definitely created by a Master Craftsman. I was stunned at all the incredible details I had missed during my initial cursory glance. I spoke a prayer of forgiveness for my impulsiveness. I told the Lord that I loved Him and wanted to stay and admire His work as long as He would allow me.

January 1998: The Second Vision

The first vision replayed and now continued to part two. I had examined the room for days and hours in all its glory. Jesus was in the room with me now. He took me by the hand and led me to the dreaded doors. As He opened the doors, there was solid ground. Going through the doors still frightened me because I had become even more comfortable in the room. He held my hand tightly reassuring me of His presence.

With confidence, He stepped out and led me up a lush hillside. When we got to the top there was a cross. I knew it was His cross and tears started to flow down my face. Leaning into His comforting arms, we looked out through the morning light and I pondered my future. As He turned me around to see the most incredible view, I knew that as long as I stayed close to Jesus I had nothing to fear. He whispered, "You are safe and secure. Trust me and follow me in my ways."

September 1999: The Third Vision

Visions one and two played all the way through; same as before. Part three started with me on the same hillside still holding hands with Jesus when He spoke.

"It's time to go."

"Where?" He motioned to the city below the hillside. It was nestled between the hills on the edge of the great ocean.

It was extraordinary and breathtaking rising out of the water.

"Follow Me to your work. Never forget that I will always be with you and will never forsake you." We headed down the hill together and I was overjoyed.

Words of Encouragement

But now, before I run down the streets, I'm praising Him. I'm not waiting for Him to do something before I praise Him. People all around me tell me they see me healed. There is a long list of friends, family and church family in Hawaii, Arizona, Texas, and beyond who have dreamed and described instances of me standing again and walking and running.

They see visions of me at church, outside the grocery

store, in a hotel lobby, walking up a stairway, at a wedding, or even at their homes. Each and every one is as wonderful as the next. I listen intently to every rich and precious detail as they come to tell me what they see in dreams, visions and thoughts. They see that God has accomplished, a magnificent show of His power and glory through me.

They text me, call me and tell me in person of the images they have seen; even of my Pastor throwing my cart overhead into a dumpster as the Mighty Men, my brotherhood of faithful believers, gather in a crowd around us and cheer in a powerful roar. They see me standing, running, walking and testifying to the mighty miracle working power of our glorious Creator! Even now, they are also being mentored by Jesus, Mentored by a Maverick Himself, as He gives them a glimpse into what is next.

Praise for my Maverick Mentor

Back when I was a maverick it was all about me and how wise I was in my own eyes. I realized I needed to stop thinking my way and start thinking His way. What a different perspective it has brought to my life. I learned God has a bigger picture than we do. He wants to mentor each of us and teach us. As I thought about my future every day, my bride would ask me almost every morning, "If you were free of that chair, what would you do today?" My answer was always the same. "RUN!"

(Philippians 3:13-15 - Brothers and sisters, I do not consider myself yet to have taken hold of it. But one thing I do: Forgetting what is behind and straining toward what is ahead, I press on toward the goal to win the prize for which God has called me heavenward in Christ Jesus.)

Postscript

This cowboy has ridden off into the sunset. He has been called by his Maverick Mentor to go back to where he came from and run to his heart's contentment. Glory!

To Him be all the glory, honor and praise.
Rob "Maverick" Moore
April 23, 1962 - December 14, 2014

ROB and ROBIN MOORE

Acknowledgements

This endeavor would not have moved forward without the help of a rocket scientist who compelled Rob to start the process of pouring out his life onto paper. With every road block and excuse he heard her voice saying, "So, how's that working for you? Do you want life by default or design?" Thank you, Chris Parker for asking all the right questions.

Chris gifted Rob with an introduction to the creativity of wordsmith Sylvia Dzenowski. Sylvia, you endured hours of storytelling from the master of storytellers and you listened with wide-eyed amazement every time. Thank you for your delight and perseverance in helping him deliver content to his blog and beginning to put his stories in print form.

Jeff & Kim Brewer, little did we know that after a "chance" Starbucks meeting with Rob right before his passing and then your subsequent offer to "do ANYTHING to help" would turn into a book editing adventure. Thank you so much for your excitement and belief in this legacy project. Your guidance and expertise have been invaluable.

Mighty Men of Elevate Life Church, you were the catalyst for this man to get up and be fierce every day. He knew you were watching and wondering how the heck he did it. Thank you for giving him so much hope and belief that his best days were yet to come. Your ability to see the man he was, instead of his disabilities, will forever be a gift to me. Your encouragement and love for me, your beloved brother's widow, is astounding. I am humbled in your presence.

To our incredible family of origin: parents Stan & Katy, Steve & Kay; our siblings Darby & Derek, Melissa & Melinda;

and our children Jordan Dallas (JD) & Jeremiah, Morgan & Madison Kamalei--thank you for living life with a maverick. He loved you all so dearly.

Lastly, thank you to the most fitting mentor to every maverick ever born, Jesus Christ. I am eternally grateful that you branded this man.

ABOUT THE AUTHORS

Robert Stanley Moore

As a maverick, a pastor, a mentor, and a beloved conversationalist, Rob Moore spent every day of his Christian life striving to be more like Christ. During his "Sage Years," he penned memoirs about his relationship with God, which covered everything from miracles to divine interventions, a little bit of anointing and a whole lot of blessing. Freely sharing his own lessons from his Maverick Mentor, Rob was quite a maverick mentor in his own right. Although he completed his earthly duties for the Kingdom of God, his legacy of wisdom endures well beyond his earthly body. He now lives on in the sons he raised, the men he so richly left his imprint upon, and in the pages of this book.

Robin K. Moore

Robin K. Moore is an author/illustrator/speaker. She and her husband Rob spent twenty of their thirty years of marriage on an island in the middle of the Pacific (Oahu). Their four children were raised with sand between their toes watching the sun set in the Hawaiian Islands. Robin is a Member SCBWI (Society of Children's Book Writers and Illustrators), and best selling author of "No Chicken For Joe" from the Joe Beanie Weenie series about a pound dog dachshund and his forever family. Returning the family to the Mainland for their kid's college years, Robin now resides in a suburb of Dallas, Texas.

ROB and ROBIN MOORE

www.ingramcontent.com/pod-product-compliance
Lightning Source LLC
Chambersburg PA
CBHW071420090426
42737CB00011B/1517